LEGACY
WOMAN

ADRIANA LUNA CARLOS
Editor-In-Chief, Designer
and Co-Founder

HANNA OLIVAS
Managing Editor &
Co-Founder

ADVERTISING OPPORTUNITIES

Info@SheRisesStudios.com

LEGACY WOMAN
DECEMBER 2025

SHE RISES
STUDIOS

CONTACT US

editorial@sherisesstudios.com

WWW.SHERISESSTUDIOS.COM

LETTER FROM THE EDITORS

Dear Reader,

As we close out 2025, we are reminded of a profound truth. Legacies are not built in someday. They are built in motion. They are built in the daily choices, the bold decisions, the risks taken, and the moments when a woman chooses to rise again, no matter what tried to silence her. That is why this edition of Legacy Woman Magazine is dedicated to celebrating *Legacy in Motion: Defining the Future, One Bold Move at a Time.*

Legacy Woman is not just a publication. It is a living archive of the visionaries, disruptors, and empire-builders shaping tomorrow. These are the women who turn purpose into power and power into lasting impact. Their stories become roadmaps for generations to come. This month, we honor that spirit through the extraordinary life and work of our December cover feature, **Lori Balue**, a woman whose courage, transformation, and unwavering mission embody what it means to build a legacy that lives far beyond the present moment.

Lori's journey from survival to leadership is a testament to the resilience, self-reinvention, and intentionality that define a true Legacy Woman. At 62, she is not slowing down. She is hiking rim-to-rim across the Grand Canyon, running half marathons, guiding women through metabolic restoration, and proving that purpose has no age limit. Her work through Aging Adventurously™ is not only transforming bodies. It is reshaping futures. Lori stands as an example of what happens when a woman refuses to accept decline as destiny and instead chooses to write a new chapter with conviction and clarity.

This edition celebrates women like Lori who are not waiting for permission to evolve. They are choosing impact over comfort, courage over complacency, and mission over noise. Inside these pages, you will meet women who are creating movements, reshaping industries, and uplifting communities through purpose-driven work. Their stories remind us that legacy is not defined by how loudly we arrive, but by how deeply we serve and how boldly we embody our truth.

To be featured in Legacy Woman Magazine is more than recognition. It is a declaration. A declaration that your voice matters, your vision endures, and your work shapes the world we are building together.As you read this edition, we invite you to reflect on your own legacy in motion. What story are you writing? What impact are you shaping? What bold move is calling you forward?

May this issue ignite your purpose, strengthen your courage, and remind you that your legacy is not waiting in the distance. It is already unfolding, one powerful step at a time.

Warm regards,

Adriana Luna Carlos & Hanna Olivas
Editors of Legacy Woman Magazine

Become a Managing Partner

she wins
WOMEN'S NETWORK

Join a global Movement of Visionary Women
50+ Chapters. Transformative Community. Unlimited Growth.

WHAT'S INCLUDED

- 40% commission on memberships + event bonuses
- Leadership training, toolkits & ongoing support
- VIP access to retreats, masterminds & more

Join for just

www.shewinswomensnetwork.com

Application Fee (paid only after acceptance)

AGING ADVENTUROUSLY:

HOW LORI BALUE TURNED SURVIVAL INTO A MOVEMENT

By **She Rises Studios Editorial Team**

Lori Balue did not set out to become a movement leader. She set out to live. After decades of struggling with obesity, chronic asthma, and the cycle of temporary weight loss and regain, Lori discovered a new way to live that rebuilt her body from the inside out. Today she is a Functional Diagnostic Nutrition Practitioner, founder of Aging Adventurously and the Holistic Low Carb Method, and a living example of what is possible for women over 50 who refuse to accept decline as destiny. At 62, she hikes rim-to-rim across the Grand Canyon, runs half-marathons, and teaches other women how to reclaim energy, confidence, and adventurous spirit.

Her transformation began as a search for healing rather than another diet. Lori tried supplements, strict plans, and short-term approaches that worked briefly and then failed. She relied on inhalers and a breathing machine for asthma for twenty years. It was while working in a natural food store and reading functional nutrition books that a pattern began to emerge: food and lifestyle were driving inflammation, cravings, and disease. A pivotal moment came in 2016 at the Bulletproof Conference, where conversations about biohacking and ketogenic nutrition electrified her sense of possibility. She adopted a paleo, then low-carb approach, and the changes were dramatic. Within months she lost twenty pounds, regained energy, and felt alive again. That experience shifted her purpose from personal recovery to professional calling.

Lori describes her work as a calling born from both lived experience and rigorous training. She completed Chris Kresser's ADAPT Functional Health Coaching Program and became certified in Functional Diagnostic Nutrition. From that foundation she developed Aging Adventurously, a holistic process that helps women reverse prediabetes, repair metabolism, and achieve lasting weight loss without medications or extremes. The program blends functional lab testing with a protein-forward, low-carb nutrition plan, circadian rhythm optimization, movement practices, and mindset renewal. In Lori's world, labs are not punitive; they are maps. She uses GI-MAP, DUTCH, HTMA, MRT and other tests to reveal hidden drivers of fatigue, inflammation, and metabolic dysfunction, and then builds personalized plans that restore function and freedom.

What Lori emphasizes most is that midlife struggles are rarely the result of failure. They are signals. Stress and cortisol dysregulation, gut inflammation, mineral depletion, blood sugar instability, and hormone metabolism issues are common root causes she uncovers through testing. Once the data is revealed, the work becomes precise. Lori's Holistic Low Carb Method does more than restrict calories. It reduces inflammation and visceral fat by removing foods and chemicals that trigger immune responses, nourishing clients with the right fats and a protein focus, and aligning eating times with circadian rhythms. The result is metabolic repair that supports strength, mobility, and life, not just a number on the scale.

Lori's approach is deeply practical. She introduced the idea of the food bridge, a step that transitions women away from processed foods toward satisfying low-carb alternatives. Her Aging Beautifully and Adventurously recipe book gives women swaps that retrain the palette and restore joy in eating. Weekly accountability calls stabilize blood sugar, naturally activate appetite regulation, and quiet cravings. Functional labs then clarify the specific issues for each woman so that the plan is not guesswork but a targeted reset.

Movement plays a central role in Lori's philosophy. Once a survival tool for her, movement evolved into medicine. She recalls early days when a child on the street pointed and taunted, and when a partner's question about weight became the spark for change. Walking pulled her out of helplessness and into possibility. Over time that simple movement grew into training for life. Lori learned that sunlight, grounding, midday movement, and resistance exercises improve circadian rhythms, reduce cortisol, and rewire metabolism. Today she uses movement to build mitochondria, preserve muscle, and create joy. Her goals are not extremes; they are real life milestones: hiking, playing with grandchildren, running errands without pain. Movement is how she trains for all of it.

Lori's clinical experience and client stories bring her philosophy to life. She shares the story of Leslie, a woman who arrived after 16 years of depression, fatigue, and daily pain while following a rigid diet.

Functional testing revealed mineral depletion, H. pylori and candida, and cortisol dysregulation. By restoring minerals, supporting cortisol, and addressing gut infections, Leslie regained the ability to attend events, tackle physical tasks, and find joy. She now swims on a masters team and travels independently. Stories like Leslie's are emblematic of Lori's claim that midlife is not a mystery but a map. When women look at the data, the body says what it needs, and healing becomes possible.

Beyond labs and movement, Lori's work addresses the mental barriers that keep women stuck. Many women over 50 have been told that symptoms are inevitable, or that their bodies are simply succumbing to age. Lori uses her lived experience to dismantle that narrative. She helps women build vision, provide accountability, and create daily rituals that support metabolic repair. Her first-step advice is practical and accessible: combine food into three balanced, protein-forward meals, reduce snacking, and get outside within an hour of sunrise to reset the circadian rhythm. These small shifts produce measurable change quickly, which in turn creates motivation and momentum.

At the center of Aging Adventurously is a joyful, stubborn refusal to accept decline. Lori reframes aging as an adventure, not a series of losses. She envisions Sedona retreats that combine nature immersion, metabolic coaching, and vision building. She wants to guide women down the Bright Angel Trail and train them for life through practical hikes and metabolic resets. Her long term goals include building a global community where women do not just talk about health but live it, where movement is the default and low-carb nutrition sustains energy into the nineties.

Lori's daily life reflects her work. She begins with sunrise light, grounding on dirt, and protein-first meals that include at least thirty grams of protein. Movement is woven through her day in walks, resistance training, and weekend hikes. She dims lights at sunset, protects sleep, and keeps mindset anchored in service and gratitude. For Lori, the goal is longevity with purpose: to be strong enough to pick up grandchildren and mobile enough to keep adventuring.

Her message is both simple and radical: healing starts with data, and it sticks with rhythm. When women stop guessing and start testing, and when they align nutrition with nature and movement, they stop fighting their bodies and begin to partner with them. Aging Adventurously is not about chasing youth. It is about reclaiming vitality, curiosity, and daring. Lori Balue's life is proof that transformation takes time, patience, and consistent choices, and that the second half of life can be the most adventurous chapter yet.

Connect With Lori

www.instagram.com/loribalueweightloss
www.facebook.com/lori.balue.2025
www.youtube.com/@loribalueweightloss
www.linkedin.com/in/loribaluefdn
www.loribalue.com

BRUNCH & BOSS UP™

Brunch & Boss Up™ is not your average talk show—it's a bold, live YouTube experience filmed at high-energy brunch events across the U.S. Designed for the modern entrepreneur, each episode brings together a rotating cast of inspiring business owners, thought leaders, and creatives for real, unfiltered conversations in front of a live audience.

Expect candid stories, fun games, and breakthrough moments—served with mimosas, good food, and great company.

A LIVE BRUNCH SHOW ABOUT REAL ENTREPRENEURS, REAL STORIES, AND BOSS-LEVEL ENERGY

WHERE ELSE CAN YOU SIP MIMOSAS, SHARE STORIES, AND SPARK BREAKTHROUGHS OVER BRUNCH?

Brunch & Boss Up™ is a bold new live YouTube show filmed at high-energy brunch events across the U.S.—where entrepreneurs, creatives, and change-makers come together to eat, laugh, connect, and rise.

Hosted by Hanna Olivas and Adriana Luna Carlos, founders of She Rises Studios and FENIX TV, the show is a natural extension of their mission to empower women globally through storytelling, media, and community. Together, they create spaces where women feel seen, heard, and inspired to lead boldly.

Each episode is filmed in front of a live audience and features a rotating lineup of powerhouse guests who bring their stories, insights, and unfiltered truths to the table. It's where personality meets purpose, and where mimosas meet the mic.

From hilarious games and real conversations to unexpected breakthroughs, Brunch & Boss Up™ is equal parts fun, fierce, and uplifting.

Think Red Table Talk meets UpDating—with a shot of a mimosa and a whole lot of hustle.

Hosted by dynamic duo Hanna Olivas and Adriana Luna Carlos, the show brings their signature energy and heart to every city it touches. Each event is designed to celebrate connection, elevate voices, and create space for meaningful growth and collaboration.

Want to be part of the cast?

We're looking for 4–6 bold, dynamic entrepreneurs in each city to join the show.

As a featured cast member, you'll be:

- On stage, live with our hosts
- Part of the games, challenges, and conversations
- Featured on YouTube and across our social media
- Celebrated for your energy, personality, and story—not just your business

Brunch & Boss Up™ is coming to cities near you.

APPLY TO BE IN THE CAST

Info@SheRisesStudios.com

INDRA NOOYI:

CRAFTING A LEGACY OF LEADERSHIP AND PURPOSE

By **She Rises Studios Editorial Team**

© CT WOMEN'S HALL OF FAME

As 2025 comes to a close, **Legacy Woman™ Magazine** turns its focus to the leaders who are shaping the future with vision, courage, and impact. In this special year-end edition, *Legacy in Motion*, we celebrate women who are not only defining industries but also laying the groundwork for a more inclusive, equitable, and purpose-driven world. Among these trailblazers stands **Indra Nooyi**, former CEO and Chair of PepsiCo, whose influence continues to resonate across global business and leadership circles.

Nooyi's career is a masterclass in **strategic, purpose-driven leadership**. During her tenure at PepsiCo, she transformed the company with a forward-thinking vision that balanced growth with responsibility, emphasizing nutrition, sustainability, and long-term innovation. Her leadership style was defined not only by business acumen but by an unwavering commitment to inclusivity, equity, and mentorship. Today, she extends that influence through her board roles, mentorship initiatives, and speaking engagements, proving that true legacy is built through both achievement and advocacy.

What sets Nooyi apart is her focus on **building a lasting impact that goes beyond profit margins**. She consistently emphasizes the importance of aligning business decisions with broader societal needs. Her approach exemplifies the core theme of *Legacy in Motion*: success is measured not only by immediate results, but by the enduring structures, systems, and cultures a leader creates. For aspiring women leaders, Nooyi's journey demonstrates that vision and purpose can coexist with operational excellence and strategic growth.

Mentorship is another pillar of Nooyi's enduring influence. Throughout her career and into her post-CEO endeavors, she has actively guided and championed women in business, providing insights, resources, and encouragement to the next generation of leaders. By modeling **inclusive leadership**, she empowers others to step into positions of influence, amplifying diverse voices that might otherwise go unheard. In the context of Universal Human Rights Month, her dedication to equity and opportunity resonates deeply, illustrating that leadership is about opening doors as much as walking through them.

Nooyi's legacy also reflects **adaptability and resilience**, traits crucial for women navigating today's complex global business landscape. She has continually embraced change, from transforming product portfolios at PepsiCo to engaging with international markets and evolving consumer needs.

Her story teaches that bold moves, grounded in careful planning and ethical consideration, create momentum that lasts well beyond an individual's tenure.

Moreover, Nooyi champions the integration of **purpose with performance**, demonstrating that companies can thrive while contributing positively to society. Her focus on sustainable business practices, corporate responsibility, and ethical leadership reinforces a critical lesson for women building their legacies: success is amplified when it serves a higher purpose and leaves a meaningful imprint on communities and industries.

In the pages of *Legacy Woman™ Magazine*, Nooyi's journey serves as a blueprint for creating **legacy in motion**. From boardrooms to mentorship circles, she exemplifies how intentional leadership, guided by principle and vision, can transform organizations and inspire generations. Her story reminds readers that leadership is not a title—it's an ongoing commitment to impact, empowerment, and ethical excellence.

As the year concludes and 2026 approaches, Indra Nooyi stands as a testament to the enduring power of visionary leadership. She illustrates that legacy is not a static milestone but a dynamic force, continuously shaping the future through thoughtful action, mentorship, and purpose-driven decision-making. For women aspiring to lead, innovate, and influence, Nooyi's example underscores a profound truth: the most lasting legacies are built today, through bold moves, meaningful contributions, and the courage to redefine what leadership can achieve.

Indra Nooyi embodies a leadership legacy that is active, intentional, and inspiring—proof that true impact is measured by the lives we touch, the cultures we shape, and the opportunities we create for the next generation of leaders.

www.sherisesstudios.com

© AMERICAN ACADEMY OF ARTS AND SCIENCES

GRAB YOUR COPY NOW

The Bible reminds us in Romans 12:2: "Do not conform to the pattern of this world, but be transformed by the renewing of your mind." This renewal is exactly what brain science supports. Start by taking a deep breath and deciding, "Today will be better." Repeat uplifting scriptures or affirmations that resonate with you, and watch your day transform.

For guided meditations and coaching that helps you rewire your brain quickly, explore the resources on our website and our YouTube channel. Make today count. Choose your mindset.

 WWW.ERICAELLIOTT.COM   WWW.YOUTUBE.COM/@WARRIORHEARTHEALINGHEARTS

Brand Up

Your indispensable guide to high-octane success in the modern workplace as you navigate your budding career.

Available at the following retailers

amazon BARNES&NOBLE Walmart TARGET

NGOZI OKONJO-IWEALA:

GLOBAL LEADERSHIP WITH PURPOSE AND IMPACT

By **She Rises Studios Editorial Team**

As 2025 draws to a close, **Legacy Woman™ Magazine** celebrates women whose influence transcends borders, industries, and expectations. In this special year-end edition, *Legacy in Motion*, we honor trailblazers whose bold decisions and unwavering vision are shaping the future of leadership. Among these global leaders stands **Ngozi Okonjo-Iweala**, Director-General of the World Trade Organization (WTO), whose career is a testament to transformative leadership, economic inclusion, and sustainable development.

Okonjo-Iweala's appointment as the **first woman and first African Director-General of the WTO** marked a historic moment in global governance. She stepped into a role traditionally dominated by men, leading with clarity, courage, and a commitment to equitable trade. Her leadership exemplifies the power of vision married with action — proving that influence at the highest levels is not just about strategy, but about advocating for fairness, inclusivity, and shared prosperity on a global scale.

Her tenure at the WTO demonstrates a mastery of **purpose-driven leadership**. Okonjo-Iweala has consistently championed policies that prioritize economic development, particularly for marginalized and developing nations. By addressing systemic inequities in global trade, she empowers countries to participate meaningfully in the world economy. This approach aligns with the *Legacy in Motion* ethos: lasting impact is measured not merely by personal or institutional achievement, but by the opportunities created for others to thrive.

A cornerstone of Okonjo-Iweala's legacy is her **commitment to inclusion and equity**. Beyond her groundbreaking role, she has tirelessly advocated for gender equality, youth empowerment, and the elevation of voices often excluded from economic decision-making. In a world where systemic barriers still persist, her leadership models how thoughtful, inclusive governance can drive both fairness and global progress. Her work underscores that legacy is not only about the milestones achieved but also about the transformative structures and policies one leaves behind.

Okonjo-Iweala's career also reflects **resilience and adaptability**, qualities essential for navigating complex global systems. From her previous leadership roles as Nigeria's Finance Minister to her stewardship of international economic policy, she has consistently tackled crises with integrity and foresight. Her ability to balance diplomacy, strategic thinking, and ethical responsibility illustrates that bold decisions can create meaningful change — even in the most challenging environments.

Moreover, Okonjo-Iweala demonstrates that **sustainable development and leadership are inseparable**. She advocates for trade and economic policies that consider environmental, social, and cultural impacts, emphasizing that long-term success must harmonize profit, growth, and the well-being of communities worldwide. Her perspective reminds leaders that influence carries responsibility, and that thoughtful decision-making can drive systemic transformation with lasting benefits.

In the pages of *Legacy Woman™ Magazine*, Okonjo-Iweala's story serves as a blueprint for **legacy on a global scale**. She embodies the principle that leadership is active, inclusive, and purpose-driven — a reminder that courage, vision, and ethical action create ripples far beyond individual achievements. Her journey reinforces the magazine's message that legacy is built in real-time, through deliberate choices, strategic foresight, and the empowerment of others.

As we enter 2026, Ngozi Okonjo-Iweala stands as a symbol of **world-changing leadership**. She demonstrates that true legacy combines expertise with empathy, strategy with inclusivity, and ambition with purpose. For women aspiring to lead across industries and borders, her example illuminates a path where influence is measured not only by authority but by the positive impact one leaves on the world. **Ngozi Okonjo-Iweala proves that the most enduring legacies are those that transform systems, uplift communities, and redefine what it means to lead with courage, integrity, and vision.**

www.sherisesstudios.com

SARA MENKER:

INNOVATING A LEGACY OF GLOBAL IMPACT

By **She Rises Studios Editorial Team**

In this edition of **Legacy Woman™ Magazine**, celebrating *Legacy in Motion*, we spotlight women whose vision and innovation are reshaping industries and communities worldwide. Among these trailblazers stands **Sara Menker**, Founder and CEO of **Gro Intelligence**, whose work exemplifies how technology, data, and purpose-driven leadership can create a legacy that transforms lives on a global scale.

Menker's journey began with a deep awareness of **global food insecurity and agricultural inefficiencies**. Recognizing that access to accurate, timely data could revolutionize decision-making in agriculture and economics, she founded Gro Intelligence — an AI-powered platform designed to analyze and predict trends in food supply, climate impact, and market dynamics. Through this visionary approach, Menker has positioned technology as a **catalyst for meaningful social and economic change**, demonstrating that innovation and humanity are not mutually exclusive.

Her work has earned international recognition, including being named to **TIME's 100 Most Influential People** list. But beyond accolades, Menker's influence lies in her **ability to translate complex data into actionable insights** that governments, corporations, and NGOs can use to make informed decisions — ultimately reducing food insecurity and supporting sustainable global growth. Her vision proves that leadership grounded in **purpose and expertise** can have far-reaching, measurable impact.

Menker embodies the essence of **living legacy leadership**. She combines entrepreneurial ambition with social responsibility, showing that business and innovation can coexist with global stewardship. Her platform demonstrates that **data-driven solutions, when aligned with human-centered goals, have the power to reshape systems and empower communities** across continents. This approach underscores the core principle of *Legacy in Motion*: leaving a lasting mark through meaningful, tangible action.

A defining feature of Menker's leadership is her commitment to **bridging technology and humanity**. She recognizes that AI and analytics are tools, not ends in themselves, and uses them to **address some of the world's most pressing challenges** — from climate change and crop prediction to economic stability. By combining visionary thinking with empathy and strategic foresight, Menker shows that innovation guided by purpose creates not just progress, but enduring impact.

Her journey also offers a blueprint for aspiring women leaders. Menker demonstrates that **ambition, intellect, and social consciousness** can intersect to create transformative change. She inspires a generation to leverage technology responsibly, think globally, and prioritize solutions that benefit humanity as a whole. In doing so, she models a form of leadership where **success is measured not solely by profit, but by the positive legacy one leaves for future generations**.

In the pages of *Legacy Woman™ Magazine*, Sara Menker's work illustrates how **visionary thinking, technological innovation, and unwavering commitment to social impact define modern legacy leadership**.

Her mission to tackle global food insecurity exemplifies how one leader's foresight and dedication can generate ripples of change felt around the world.

As we look toward 2026, Menker continues to redefine what it means to lead with purpose. She reminds us that a true legacy is not simply a record of achievements but **a living, evolving impact that improves lives and inspires action across industries and nations**.

Sara Menker proves that **innovation, empathy, and strategic vision are the cornerstones of a legacy in motion — one that bridges technology and humanity to build a better, more sustainable world**.

www.sherisesstudios.com

© TIME MAGAZINE

WHITNEY WOLFE HERD:

REDEFINING CONNECTION, INNOVATION, AND MODERN LEGACY

By **She Rises Studios Editorial Team**

As 2025 comes to a close, **Legacy Woman™ Magazine** spotlights women whose bold vision and innovative leadership are reshaping industries and communities. In this edition, *Legacy in Motion*, we honor trailblazers turning ambition into impact. Among these transformative figures stands **Whitney Wolfe Herd**, founder and CEO of Bumble,

whose entrepreneurial journey exemplifies empowerment-driven innovation and modern legacy-building in the tech world.

Wolfe Herd's story is one of **disruption and vision**.

From launching Bumble as a dating app that prioritized women's agency to leading it through one of the most successful woman-led tech IPOs, she has consistently challenged conventional norms. Her mission has always extended beyond business metrics: she sought to create a platform where connection, respect, and empowerment were at the core. This purpose-centered approach not only transformed online dating but also inspired a broader cultural shift in how women are represented and heard in technology.

A key aspect of Wolfe Herd's leadership is her **commitment to empowerment**. By prioritizing inclusivity and safety in digital spaces, she has built a company culture rooted in respect and equity. Under her guidance, Bumble expanded beyond dating, introducing professional networking and friendship-building features — a move that underscores her belief in holistic connectivity. Wolfe Herd demonstrates that **true innovation integrates social impact with growth strategy**, proving that businesses can thrive while uplifting communities.

Her journey also highlights the importance of **resilience and courage** in modern entrepreneurship. Navigating the challenges of building a tech company as a young woman in a male-dominated industry required determination, strategic foresight, and an unwavering belief in her mission. Wolfe Herd's willingness to challenge industry norms and prioritize values over conformity illustrates a modern blueprint for leadership: success is measured not only by profit but by influence, culture, and societal contribution.

Wolfe Herd's expansion of Bumble into professional and social networking arenas further reflects her **forward-thinking vision**. She recognizes that legacy is built not solely on the foundations of a single product but on the evolution of an ecosystem that empowers users at multiple levels. By creating spaces where women, men, and communities can engage meaningfully, Wolfe Herd exemplifies how thoughtful innovation can amplify both business impact and social good.

Beyond her company, Wolfe Herd has become a **symbol of modern entrepreneurial leadership**. She embodies a new standard in which disruption is aligned with responsibility, innovation is paired with empowerment, and success is leveraged to create tangible change. Her story reinforces the idea that legacy is not simply about what one achieves, but about the systems, opportunities, and cultural shifts one leaves in motion.

In the pages of *Legacy Woman™ Magazine*, Wolfe Herd's journey serves as an inspiring example for women and entrepreneurs striving to lead with purpose. She shows that building a legacy requires more than ambition: it demands **intentional action, empathy, and the courage to reshape industries while uplifting others**. Her leadership demonstrates that a business can be both profitable and socially transformative when grounded in clear values and a forward-looking vision.

As 2026 approaches, Whitney Wolfe Herd continues to redefine what it means to lead in tech. Through empowerment-driven innovation, inclusive platforms, and visionary strategy, she illustrates that **legacy in the modern age is built through disruption, community, and meaningful connection**.

Whitney Wolfe Herd proves that **redefining industries, amplifying voices, and fostering connection are the cornerstones of a legacy that transcends the boardroom, leaving a lasting imprint on culture, business, and society.**

www.sherisesstudios.com

© THE NEW YORK TIMES

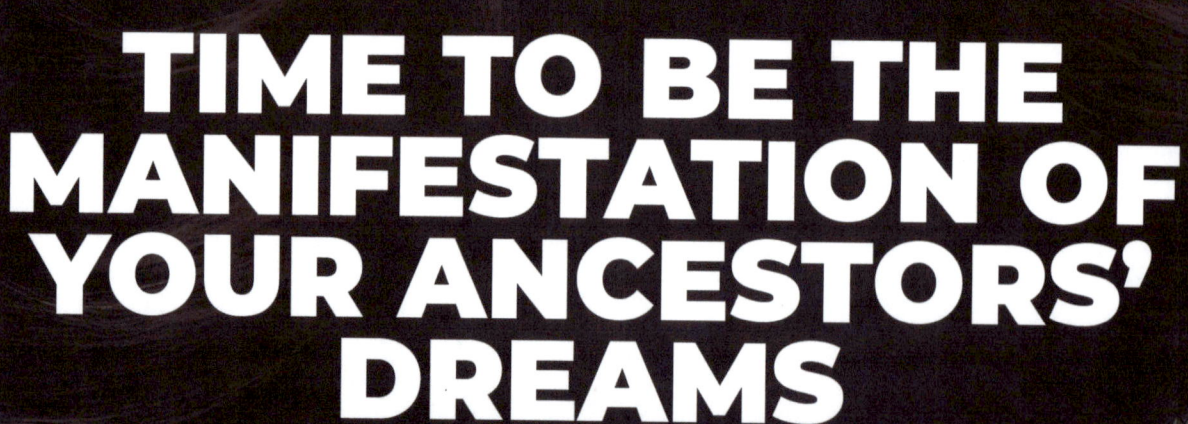

TIME TO BE THE MANIFESTATION OF YOUR ANCESTORS' DREAMS

By **Dr. Gabrielle Thomas Booker**

Legacy is more than memory—it is momentum. The women who came before you, whether you knew their names or only felt their echoes, carved pathways through obstacles you will never have to face. They stitched dignity into the fabric of their families, held hope through storms, and dreamed boldly even when the world denied them space to breathe. Today, you stand in the light of possibilities they never saw, and there is profound power in recognizing that this moment —your moment—is part of a lineage of resilience.

To be the manifestation of your ancestors' dreams is not simply a poetic idea; it is a lived truth. Every opportunity you grasp, every boundary you break, every version of yourself you allow to bloom is tethered to someone who once imagined more for the generations that would follow. In kitchens, in fields, in boardrooms they never entered, and in stories that have faded with time, they whispered visions of a future in which the daughters of their daughters could rise unencumbered.

In a world where we often feel pressured to achieve, perform, or constantly measure our progress, it helps to remember that your existence is already extraordinary. You are living in a reality that past generations could not fully access—whether that means owning your ambitions, having autonomy over your voice, or choosing who you become. Simply by inhabiting your life with intention, you honor a lineage of women who walked so you could run.

Yet manifestation is not passive. It invites you to participate in shaping the future with the same determination your ancestors showed in shaping the present. This may look like pursuing the education they were denied, starting the business they didn't have the resources to imagine, speaking truths they had to swallow, or raising a family in tenderness they were never allowed to feel. It might look like building wealth, rewriting family narratives, claiming self-care without guilt, or stepping boldly into leadership in spaces that once excluded you.

One of the most powerful forms of legacy-building is healing. Many women inherit not only strength, but also silence—patterns of survival that protected one generation but limit the next. When you choose therapy, set boundaries, embrace softness, or refuse to shrink yourself, you are not breaking from your lineage; you are elevating it. Healing is a profound act of devotion to the women who carried burdens so you could put them down.

But legacy is not only about struggle. It is also about joy. Your ancestors laughed, sang, celebrated, loved deeply, and held onto beauty in the midst of hardship. Joy is part of your inheritance. When you allow yourself to experience delight—to dance, to rest, to create, to express—you honor not only their sacrifices but also their humanity. You become a continuation of their light, not just their labor.

Being the manifestation of their dreams means understanding that you are not alone. You are surrounded by generations of wisdom, courage, and quiet revolution. Their stories live in your choices. Their hopes live in your heartbeat. Their resilience lives in every step you take toward a life that reflects freedom, abundance, and authenticity.

This is your time. Not only to honor where you come from, but to expand what is possible for those who will follow you. You are the dream realized—and the dream in progress. You are the evidence that their prayers survived, their hopes endured, and their love arrived in the world wrapped in your skin.

So walk boldly, Legacy Woman. Speak your truth, claim your brilliance, and shape a future that would make your ancestors proud. You are their gift to tomorrow—and the world has been waiting for you to step fully into your power.

Connect With Dr. Gabrielle

@cmalegacymentoringprogram
www.facebook.com/share/17Sq3dk1Vo

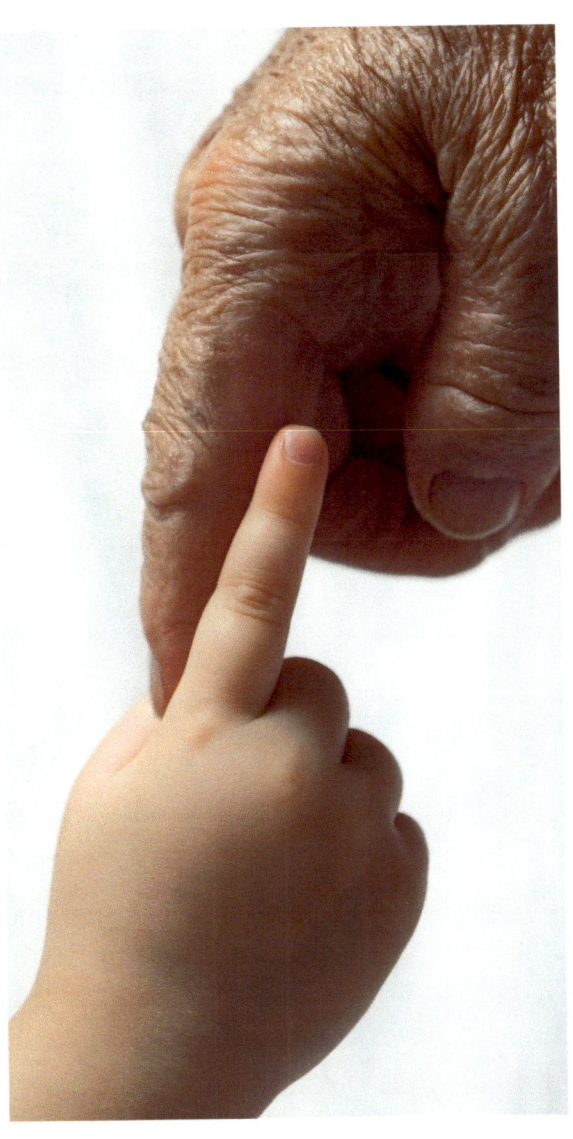

JOIN THE SHE RISES STUDIOS COMMUNITY

SCAN TO JOIN

Daily motivation, expert insights, and sisterhood support come together in one empowering space. Connect, empower, and thrive—whether you're an entrepreneur, professional, or simply seeking inspiration, this is your place to grow!

You don't have to do it alone—let's rise together!

THE SHE RISES STUDIOS
PODCAST

Each episode of the She Rises Studios Podcast delivers real stories, expert insights, and actionable strategies to help you step into your power and create the life you desire. This isn't just a podcast—it's your roadmap to confidence, success, and purpose.

Through powerful interviews with trailblazing entrepreneurs, thought leaders, and inspiring women, we dive deep into conversations that spark growth, fuel ambition, and ignite your potential. If you're ready to rise higher and live boldly, you're in the right place.

SUBSCRIBE NOW AND START YOUR JOURNEY TO EMPOWERMENT!

LIVING FROM SOUL:

HOW SCIENTIFIC SPIRITUALITY IS TRANSFORMING WOMEN'S LIVES THROUGH THE FOUR WORLDS PERSONALITY FRAMEWORK & NOBLE ENERGY MAPS®

By **Dr. Eleanor Haspel-Portner, Ph.D.**

In every generation, women emerge who connect what once seemed impossible. For me, that connection has always been the intersection of rigorous science, deep spirituality, and the profound dignity of the human soul. My life's work, spanning over fifty years of clinical practice, research, authorship, and global teaching, focused on understanding the structure of consciousness in a way that is both scientifically valid and spiritually empowering.

From the outside, I am a clinical psychologist, social scientist, psychic, and best-selling author. But at the core, I am a woman dedicated to helping others live their fullest expression of who God designed them to be. Through my signature systems, **The Four Worlds Personality Framework** and **Noble Energy Maps® (NEM)**, I guide people to understand their true nature, navigate life with clarity and truth, and live from the soul with purpose, confidence, and faith.

A Lifetime of Scientific Inquiry Rooted in Spirit

My journey began at the University of Chicago, where I trained under pioneers in psychology, anthropology, and the study of consciousness. While deeply grounded in empirical science, I always felt called to explore the higher architecture of human experience, the kind that traditional psychology could hint at but not fully capture.

That search eventually led me to co-author 13 books with Ra Uru Hu and to conduct the only large-scale statistical analysis ever performed on the Human Design system. My dataset of more than 45,000 cases, including 30,000 clinically analyzed matched designs, revealed profound truths about the structure of human consciousness, truths that ultimately formed the scientific foundation of **Noble Energy Maps®**, the trademarked and validated successor to traditional Human Design.

NEM is not theoretical. It is tested, replicated, and proven across decades of research. At the same time, it is deeply spiritual, rooted in the sacred geometry of the authentic Human Design Body Graph, the Kabbalistic Tree of Life, astrology, I-Ching harmonics, and the energetic imprints that govern human behavior. It is the first system of its kind to unite faith, science, and soul in a coherent, reliable model.

The Four Worlds: A Framework for Authentic Living

At the heart of my work is the **Four Worlds Personality Framework**, a model that helps people understand the multidimensional nature of their consciousness:

- **Mental/Waking World:** the world of thought, logic, and conscious decision-making.
- **Emotional/Angelic World:** the realm of feeling, intuition, and inner attunement.
- **Physical/Biological World:** the tangible body, instincts, and the rhythms that shape daily life.
- **Spiritual/Archetypal World:** the deepest layer of the soul's purpose, destiny, and divine imprinting.
- **Integrated World:** the point of synthesis where all four levels align and the true self emerges.

Women often learn to suppress aspects of themselves, to be rational yet not emotional, spiritual yet not intellectual, decisive yet not assertive. The Four Worlds integrates that fragmentation.

Noble Energy Maps® reveal the whole person. They restore dignity to our complexity and help women reclaim the integrated strength God intended.

A Legacy of Empowerment and Truth

Whether I am mentoring high-level entrepreneurs, speaking to global audiences, or guiding clients through the Noble Energy Maps®, my mission stays the same: to empower people, especially women, to step into their power, faith, and clarity by understanding themselves at the deepest level possible.

Scientific spirituality is not an abstraction. It is a lived path. It is the meeting place of truth and grace. Through my work with Noble Energy Maps® and the Four Worlds, I offer women a blueprint to navigate life from their soul's intelligence—not from fear, confusion, or conditioning.

In a world that often pulls us away from our true nature, my calling is to help women return to their radiant, grounded, purposeful, and whole Self.

Connect With Dr. Eleanor

www.nobleenergywellness.com
www.linkedin.com/in/eleanor-haspel-portner-phd
www.facebook.com/EleanorHaspelPortnerPhD
www.instagram.com/nobleenergywellness
www.x.com/ByndHumanDesign
www.tiktok.com/@noble.energy.well
www.youtube.com/@nobleenergywellness/videos
www.moptu.com/dreleanor#

FROM GREY ZONES TO GLORIOUS THIRD ACTS:
HOW I TURNED CHAOS INTO CALLING

By **Kathryn Traff**

That 17-hour hospital day still haunts me like a vivid dream —the fluorescent lights humming, monitors shrieking, me sprinting between operating rooms while a surgical imaging system and computer network crashed mid-case. Phones exploded; surgeons barked demands. I was the lone bridge between tech teams who froze without me. Burnout shadowed every step, though I didn't name it then. Amid the frenzy, a whisper promised: Just survive today, then reward yourself with that favorite glass of wine—price no object.

Four years later, I'm unrecognizable. As The Unstuck Strategist, I coach midlife women—physicians shifting to holistic care, non-profit executives, faith-driven professionals—out of their own grey zones. Late-night scrolling, emotional eating, retail therapy bandaids, or one glass of wine sliding into three? They're not flaws; they're signals. With 17 years in neuroscience, I decode those signals like brain scans.

My pivot began boldly. I quit alcohol cold. Then, with zero backup plan, I walked from the career that defined me for 17 years. To fill the void, I hit my apartment's free gym at 5 a.m. in decade-old cycling gloves and five-year-old leggings, vowing peak fitness by 60. No frills—just determination and a flicker of faith. That *"start where you are"* ethos birthed Kathryn Traff Coaching and Ministries. I fused hospital-honed neuroscience with Scripture to craft REVIVE™: a roadmap to clarity, confidence, and calling.

REVIVE isn't theory; it's lived experience. Release draining habits. Embrace your God-given identity. Visualize a vibrant future. Integrate mindset and action. Value community. Execute with joy. I was client zero—applying every step to rebuild my life. Then came miracles: a physician trading burnout for a flourishing holistic practice; a non-profit leader reclaiming her voice after decades of people-pleasing.

Grey zones flourish in secrecy, hissing lies: Too old. Too late. Worth equals output. Beautiful Soul, that's fiction. Your value was etched by your Creator before any struggle. I know—I chained myself to achievement, masking fatigue as drive, until faith shattered the illusion.

Ditching high-stakes security wasn't pretty. Sleepless nights wondered if coaching and speaking were delusions. Yet courage sparked momentum. I co-authored my first book, joined David Bayer's elite coaching team, and grew a global community on YouTube—none scripted on my old vision board. They bloomed when I unleashed my ENFP spark, Pisces intuition, and Manifesting Generator flow.

Today I around the country, lead workshops from Tallahassee to afar, and foster shame-free circles. My ministry marries neuroscience and Scripture, revealing them as partners in wholeness. The thrill? Seeing clients radiate in their third acts. One confessed, *"Kathryn, transitions now feel like invitations, not interruptions."*

If you're nodding in your grey zone, listen: Adversity is soil for your next bloom. Begin now. Dust off those old gloves —literal or figurative—and move. Faith plus one step ignites momentum. Your gifts ache to serve. Your story isn't finished; it's unfolding.

As a bestselling author and brain health mentor, I invite you. Join my community, book a session, or await my next book. Together, let's transform your catalyst into a masterpiece. The world awaits your unstuck, unstoppable light.

Kathryn Traff is The Unstuck Strategist, a neuroscience-based coach, speaker, and founder of Kathryn Traff Coaching and Ministries. She empowers midlife women to overcome grey zone habits and embrace purpose-filled transitions. Connect at *kathryntraffcoaching.com.*

Connect With Kathryn

www.linkedin.com/in/kathryntraff
www.survival2revival.com
www.youtube.com/@KathrynTraffCoaching
www.x.com/KathrynTraff
www.instagram.com/kathryntraffcoaching
www.facebook.com/share/19Wh2UCDd2

WAKE UP TO YOUR POWER:

HOW REFLECTION AND SELF-AWARENESS HELP WOMEN LEAD WITH CONFIDENCE

By **Marci Hopkins**

We live in a world that moves so quickly that many women forget to pause long enough to hear the most important voice in their lives: their own. Confidence isn't something we inherit; it's something we build. It grows from self-awareness, honest reflection, and the choice to honor our worth every single day.

As the creator and host of Wake Up with Marci, I spend each week interviewing thought leaders, healers, change-makers, and everyday women who have transformed their

lives from the inside out. No matter their background or story, one truth always rises to the surface: empowerment begins when we stop abandoning ourselves and start paying attention to what we truly feel and need. Reflection isn't indulgent, it's self-leadership. And when we learn to lead ourselves, we naturally lead others with clarity, compassion, and courage.

In my own journey, which I share in my award-winning book Chaos to Clarity:

Seeing the Signs and Breaking the Cycles, reflection was the turning point. For years, I lived on autopilot, chasing approval and silencing my own voice. When I finally turned inward, I began to heal old wounds, break generational patterns, and reclaim my identity. That inner awakening became the foundation of my confidence and ultimately the heart of my work.

Reflection Reveals What's Holding You Back

Many women carry old stories: perfectionism, past trauma, comparison, guilt, or the fear of not being enough. These stories quietly shape how we show up, what we say yes to, and how confidently we lead.

Through reflection, we start to understand:
- Why we overextend
- Why boundaries feel uncomfortable
- Why we shrink to keep the peace
- Why we seek validation instead of trusting our voice

Self-awareness shines a light on these patterns. Once we see them clearly, we can choose differently and choice is where confidence begins.

Awareness Helps You Lead Authentically

Leadership is not about perfection; it's about presence. When a woman knows her strengths, values, and emotional landscape, she leads from authenticity rather than expectation.

You become a woman who:
- Speaks truth with steady confidence
- Sets boundaries without guilt
- Makes grounded decisions
- Creates environments where others feel seen and safe

People follow leaders who know themselves and trust themselves.

Reflection Builds Emotional Resilience

Confidence doesn't mean we stop feeling fear. It means we learn how to keep moving with intention. Reflection practices like journaling, meditation, gratitude, and mindful check-ins strengthen the emotional resilience needed to navigate challenges.

Reflection helps us:
- Recover quickly from setbacks
- Stay centered under pressure
- Separate our emotions from others' expectations
- Hold space for ourselves and those we lead

Resilience is the quiet strength beneath confident leadership.

Three Daily Practices to Build Inner Confidence

1. Morning Check-In
Ask yourself: What do I need today to feel supported and grounded?

This simple question sets the tone for intentional leadership.

2. The CARE Method
A practice I share through my work:
- C — Communicate Effectively
- A — Ask for Help without Guild
- R — Reinforce Boundaries
- E — Embrace your Worth

3. Evening Gratitude & Truth
List three things you're grateful for and one truth you honored.

This builds self-trust, the foundation of confidence.

Wake Up to Your Worth

Through my show and writing, I witness every day how reflection opens the door to transformation. Women rise not by doing more, but by waking up to their worth, their wisdom, and their inner power.

When you lead yourself with awareness and intention, you don't just rise…you help others rise too.

Connect With Marci

www.wakeupwithmarci.com
www.instagram.com/wake_up_with_marci
www.youtube.com/channel/UCtv2M6RTE
YmUkLnkGgcg7Rw
www.facebook.com/wakeupwithmarci
www.linkedin.com/in/wakeupwithmarci

FROM OVERACHIEVEMENT TO OWNERSHIP:
CHOOSING MYSELF AS AN ARTIST

By **Kiayani "Kay" Douglas**

For most of my life, I believed overachievement was how I would survive. As a Black woman, I learned early that excellence wasn't optional, it was expected.

I wasn't the person who stayed late. I'm a planner by nature. I led side programs, advocated for students, and took on tasks others neglected. I said *"yes"* often, but always with careful consideration. I set clear boundaries and showed up with integrity and intention. Yet even my most reasonable limits were seen as a threat.

What I've come to realize is that many of us work inside environments that feel less like professional communities and more like high school politics in disguise. It's a silent epidemic, all women across industries vent about it online daily. The microaggressions. The favoritism. The performative wellness with no structural support. Being good at your job is never the issue. It's what happens when you're no longer easy to control.

Somewhere along the way, I stopped being seen as a full person and started being treated like a machine that couldn't break. I even blamed myself, performing ten times more than my predecessor yet receiving less recognition and more work.

Still, I held onto the part of me that mattered most: my art. I protected it quietly, working late nights, researching, reading, sketching. Then, in 2024, I was offered my fifth solo exhibition in six years. *Peace as Privilege, Justice as Resistance.* What made this show different wasn't the number of exhibitions I'd done before, but that I had completely engulfed myself in overachieving at my job. I wasn't actively seeking the opportunity. Instead, it found me at exactly the right time, a powerful reminder of my purpose and practice when I needed it most, along with things I had manifested years prior and somehow forgotten.

The exhibition featured 33 portraits from two bodies of work I built over years. These portraits honored Black life, loss, resistance, and love. They told stories that mattered. Alongside the show, I created *The People's Catalog*, a 16-page publication featuring the show and my writings, all inspired by the Black Panther Party's community model and Emory Douglas's work as Minister of Culture.

But just as the show was coming to fruition, while I was finalizing installations, fulfilling press requests, and preparing to present years of emotional labor. I was met with a harsh realization. A perceived miscommunication, really a boundary I set, spiraled into something disproportionate and punitive.

I was called into question without support, treated as a problem to fix rather than a person to understand.

It wasn't just discouraging. It was dehumanizing.

At that moment, I made a decision: I was willing to be fired before I was willing to be disrespected. I would not explain away my boundaries to preserve someone else's comfort. I would not keep shrinking to be seen as *"easy to manage."*

I stood firm in my truth, documented everything, advocated for myself, and refused to apologize for being an artist with a voice.

And instead of unraveling, I rose.

The exhibition opened to an outpouring of support. My catalog was distributed to libraries, museums, and community centers across the Berkshires in Massachusetts. I was featured in new publications, offered professional photography, and invited into spaces that celebrated my vision, not just my labor. I didn't have to choose between my practice and my profession. I chose myself, and the world responded accordingly.

Being unstoppable doesn't mean working ourselves into the ground. It means knowing when the ground beneath us is no longer worthy. It means understanding that overachievement and self-respect aren't opposites, they can coexist, but only when we're in charge of the terms.

If I could speak to the version of myself who feared honesty would cost everything, I'd say: *You were never asking for too much. You were asking the wrong people. Your work is not a burden. Your voice is not a threat. You don't have to earn protection because you deserve it.*

Today, I still work hard. I still lead. I still give. But I also rest. I draw. I research. I write. I speak up. I am no longer performing balance. I am living in alignment.

From pain, I found clarity. From clarity, I built power. That power gave me permission to be fully myself, artist, educator, mother, advocate, and beyond.

Connect With Kay

www.Iamkaydouglas.com
Instagram: @_iamkaydouglas
TikTok: @iamkaydouglas

SHE RISES
STUDIOS

$\mathcal{U}$NLEASH YOUR STORY
BECOME A PUBLISHED AUTHOR!

Have you ever dreamed of sharing your wisdom, experience, or passion with the world? **Now is your time!**

Publishing a book isn't just about writing—it's about **establishing your authority, inspiring others, and creating a lasting legac**y. Plus, with the **$138.5 billion book industry** booming, there's never been a better moment to step into the spotlight.

At **SRS Publishing**, we don't just publish books—we **elevate voices, empower authors, and create change-makers**. Our mission is to help women break barriers, amplify their stories, and thrive in the publishing world. Whether you're an entrepreneur, thought leader, or storyteller at heart, **we're here to guide you every step of the way.**

JOIN THE FASTEST-GROWING PUBLISHING HOUSE FOR WOMEN IN THE USA.

READY TO TURN YOUR DREAM INTO REALITY?

 www.SheRisesStudios.com | contact@sherisesstudios.com

FENIX TV
YOUR PLATFORM, YOUR VOICE, YOUR POWER!

STEP INTO THE SPOTLIGHT AS A HOST ON FENIX TV!

Are you ready to amplify your message, inspire others, and be part of a groundbreaking network dedicated to empowering women worldwide? FENIX TV is your platform to shine as a host, share your expertise, and connect with a global audience.

WHY HOST ON FENIX TV?

- Reach a worldwide audience passionate about empowerment
- Showcase your voice, brand, and expertise
- Join a community of inspiring leaders and changemakers
- Be part of a network that uplifts and celebrates women

Whether you dream of leading a talk show, sharing powerful stories, or educating and inspiring others—FENIX TV is where your voice matters!

SECURE YOUR SPOT TODAY!

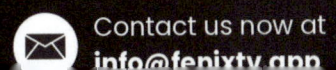
Contact us now at
info@fenixtv.app

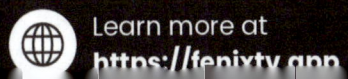
Learn more at
https://fenixtv.app

FROM PAIN TO POWER:
A Journey of Becoming Unstoppable

By **Debbie DeMarco Bennett, MA**

There was a time in my life when the chaos felt endless. I'd just lost yet another job, another chance, another version of a life I couldn't seem to hold onto. My partner at the time, the most stable relationship I'd managed up to that point, and a close friend, gently told me they couldn't keep watching me self-destruct. *"Please get help,"* they said. *"We can't keep doing this."*

I was devastated. Hopeless. Terrified.
I *had* gotten help. Years of therapy. Hospital stays. Endless efforts. And still... I felt like a lost cause.

What I couldn't see then, in the middle of the spiral, was that this would become my turning point. That heartbreak, that moment of rupture, would become the crack where the light got in.

I entered an Intensive Outpatient Program. Same clinic, same therapist, same psychiatrist. But something shifted. I decided to be radically honest, to share the thoughts I was most ashamed of, the symptoms I feared made me *"too much."* And it changed everything.

My psychiatrist gently explained that what I was describing: the disorientation, the sense of not knowing who I really was...was called *"identity disturbance."* It was one of the criteria for borderline personality disorder. She went on to assess me for the others. I remember the moment she said, *"There's a treatment that works. It's called DBT. Dialectical Behavior Therapy. We offer it here."*

Hope cracked through my despair.
Wait... other people feel like this too? There's a *name* for it? A *path* forward?

I committed. I went to every DBT group. Took notes. Did homework. Showed up, even when it hurt. I also started practicing yoga and somatic movement, meditating, and reconnecting with my own inner wisdom. For the first time, I didn't give up at the six-month mark — the point I usually spiraled. Something in me knew... this was different.

Three years later, I no longer met the criteria for BPD.
That was in 2013.
I've been in recovery ever since.

The same year, I founded *DBT Path*, an online school for emotionally sensitive people like me who were searching for hope, tools, and real connection. At the time, no such resource existed.

I wanted to be the support I had once needed, someone who gets it, who walks with you, not above you. Since then, alongside an amazing team of caring people, we've helped thousands of sensitive souls around the world. Our next class starts soon at emotionallysensitive.com.

What we offer is different. We're peer-led, trauma-informed, and heart-led. I share my story when it helps someone feel less alone on their own. I remind my students, again and again, that their sensitivity is not a flaw. It's their superpower.

To me, being *unstoppable* doesn't mean never breaking down. It means learning how to break *open* and finding your strength in the softness. It means knowing how to validate yourself. To rest without quitting. To rise with self-compassion.

If I could speak to the version of me who nearly gave up, I'd say:
  "Please hold on. One day, you'll turn this pain into purpose. You'll help others find their light, too. You'll even create a life that feels safe, full of love, and deeply meaningful. Just keep going."

Twelve years later, I've built a beautiful life…a thriving business, a supportive marriage, a cozy home filled with cats and laughter. I know who I am now, and I believe in my strength.

This is what healing can look like.

This is what becoming unstoppable feels like.

Connect With Debbie

www.emotionallysensitive.com
www.instagram.com/dbtpath
www.facebook.com/DBTPath
www.youtube.com/dbtpath

FIREFIGHTING TO FISSION ENERGY:

HOW ONE WOMAN'S BIG PIVOT IS EDUCATING THE NEXT GENERATION

By **Danielle Allen**

A Firefighter's Journey Becoming a Nuclear Energy Podcast Host

When I first started my podcast, *Naked Nuclear*, I didn't set out to become an expert or a thought leader in the nuclear industry. In fact, my background wasn't in nuclear engineering at all. I was a firefighter and paramedic, a commercial pilot, and an adventurer with a love for learning about complex systems. Nuclear energy was something I knew little about, but I was deeply curious. I wanted to understand the technology shaping our future, the people driving innovation, and the truths behind the misconceptions. So, I created a podcast, not just to share information, but to take people along on my journey of discovery.

Curiosity as the Catalyst

At the beginning, my goal was simple: learn about nuclear energy by talking to those who know it best. This industry can feel intimidating. It's filled with technical jargon, decades of history, and public skepticism. But I discovered that when you start asking questions, really asking, from a place of curiosity, doors open. Experts, engineers, and policymakers were not only willing to share their knowledge, they were excited to. Through each interview, I began to see that the nuclear energy sector is full of passionate, mission-driven individuals who believe in what they're doing.

My podcast became a platform to bridge that gap between experts and the public. Each episode pulled back another layer of the industry, making it more approachable for listeners, and for me.

People Behind the Power

One of the most surprising things I've learned is how welcoming the nuclear community is. Despite working in one of the most challenging and highly regulated industries in the world, these professionals carry an optimism that's contagious. They are innovators, problem-solvers, and educators. They've invited me into labs, control rooms, and conferences, showing me firsthand the dedication it takes to keep nuclear energy safe and relevant.

And then there are the women in this field, who have been some of the most inspiring figures I've met. Organizations like Women in Nuclear (WiN) are not only fostering support networks, they are breaking barriers and championing diversity in a sector that needs more voices at the table. Through my interviews, I've met incredible women who are leading reactor design projects, managing power plants, shaping policy, and mentoring the next generation. Their stories remind me that representation matters, and that the future of nuclear energy will be stronger because of them.

Lessons from the Journey

Podcasting has been its own adventure. It's not just hitting *"record"* and uploading an episode. It's researching, preparing, editing, and constantly learning new ways to tell stories. Along the way, I've learned three key lessons that have shaped both the podcast and me personally:

- **Start Before You're Ready**

When I launched Naked Nuclear, I didn't have everything figured out.

My audio setup was basic, my audience was small, and I was learning on the fly. But waiting for perfection would have meant never starting. Each episode taught me something new, and the process itself became my teacher.

- **Build Relationships, Not Just Content**

The heart of my podcast isn't the technology, it's the people. Building authentic relationships with guests has opened doors I didn't expect, from collaborations to mentorships. These connections have been invaluable, both for my personal growth and for my audience, who benefit from diverse voices and perspectives.

- **Stay True to Your Why**

In the world of content creation, it's easy to get caught up in numbers, downloads, likes, shares. But my mission was never about going viral, it was about learning and sharing. Keeping that at the center keeps me grounded and focused, even when growth feels slow.

Why This Mission Matters

Nuclear energy often suffers from a narrative problem. The word *"nuclear"* conjures images of accidents or weapons, rather than clean, reliable power. Through my podcast, I aim to shift that narrative, not by sugarcoating, but by educating. When people hear directly from the engineers, the plant operators, the researchers, they see the reality: nuclear energy is one of the safest, most efficient tools we have to fight climate change.

But this mission goes beyond energy. It's about inspiring curiosity, breaking down barriers, and showing that even the most complex industries are made up of people with stories worth hearing. By sharing those stories, I hope to encourage others, especially women and underrepresented voices, to step into spaces where they may feel like outsiders. Because that's how I started, and it's been life-changing.

Looking Ahead

As *Naked Nuclear* grows, my vision expands with it. I want to continue amplifying voices in the industry, from seasoned experts to students just entering the field. I'm working on larger projects, including a TV show and a scholarship fund, all tied to the same mission: making nuclear energy accessible, understandable, and exciting to the next generation.

There's still so much to learn, and that's what keeps me going. Every conversation leaves me inspired, and I hope it does the same for my listeners.

An Invitation to be Curious

If there's one thing I've learned, it's that learning doesn't happen in isolation. It happens through connection. My podcast is a space for those connections, for experts to share, for listeners to explore, and for all of us to reimagine what's possible.

To anyone curious about nuclear energy, or to anyone standing on the edge of starting something new: take the leap. Ask questions. Share what you learn. You never know where that curiosity might lead you.

Connect With Danielle

www.linkedin.com/in/danielleallen-nuclear
www.nakednuclear.com/episodes
www.open.spotify.com/show/7LB4VTrCd
HQTPGQXOzbJeQ

© MARG WOODS

PAIN TO POWER:

STORIES OF TRANSFORMATION

By **Treva Brandon Scharf**

My *"Pain to Power"* story is one of patience, resilience, and finding love later in life.

I got married for the first time at 51. Before that, I endured years of heart break, dashed hopes, and a hell of a lot of bad choices. I nearly lost myself in the process.

My single life took so many twists and turns in my 20s and 30s. First, I wasn't ready to settle down, then I was. In my 40s, every guy I dated was either separated or divorced and had no desire to jump back in. I was great to date, just not great to marry.

At 42, with a loud ticking biological clock and no potential spouse in sight, I tried to get pregnant on my own with donor sperm. That didn't work either. So, I kept dating and hoping to find my person.

I'm not a quitter. I don't give up easily. I'm a 5-time marathoner, a former fitness professional, and a driven, goal-oriented woman. I approached my romantic life like it was a quest. The more out of reach, the harder I went, the harder I was on myself.

It made me crazy that marriage alluded me. I was a bridesmaid many times over, attended countless weddings, but still, I couldn't make it happen for me.

I couldn't find my person, I couldn't make a baby, and was nearing 50. It was the perfect storm of despair. When I realized I couldn't go any lower, I did something extremely out of character:

I quit.

I gave up on marriage and the happily-ever-after. I quit the game, threw in the towel, and to be honest, I had no choice. I had no self-worth left.

When I gave up though, something strange happened: I was liberated. I released the death grip I had on love and was free.

As it turned out, giving up was the moment that changed everything.

When I said to myself: *"I'm going to be single the rest of my life, and I'm going to make it look good,"* I stepped into my true power.

I let go of the hopes and dreams, and decided to live my best life because life would go on without a husband, and I was ready to live it because I was turning 50 and fuck it.

And then I met my husband.

11 years later, I'm still marveling at my journey and the insights it gave me.

Getting married wasn't just a goal realized, it was a valuable lesson about how we view our value and worth, how we can self-sabotage, and where we can improve.

I learned that dating is less about charisma and confidence, and more about conviction: having a deep belief and trust in yourself. I learned that love takes effort, but a lot about love is out of our control. I learned that expectations are romance killers, that failure is a great teacher, and I have a new respect for serendipity, kismet, and the randomness of life.

Finding love later in life made me realize that some of us are late bloomers, and there's no shame in that. It's never too late and you're never too old to meet your person.

Getting married also changed the course of my career because I took all those years of singlehood, lived experience, pain and wisdom, and turned it into a thriving life and dating coaching business.

When it comes to helping people find love (and find themselves, which is just as important) I am unstoppable.

Connect With Treva

www.trevabrandonscharf.com
Instagram: @trevabme
www.facebook.com/treva.brandonscharf
www.linkedin.com/in/trevabrandonscharf

100
WOMEN OF IMPACT™
THE DOCUSERIES THAT AMPLIFIES WOMEN'S VOICES

We just wrapped our first taping of 100 Women of Impact™ in San Diego, and the momentum has only just begun. This powerful docuseries is shining a spotlight on extraordinary women who are shaping the future through leadership, resilience, and influence.

Be part of the movement by sharing your story in an exclusive filmed interview for the docuseries. Gain visibility through red carpet experiences, media coverage, and distribution across She Rises Studios platforms, while connecting with a global network of women making an unstoppable impact.

NEXT FILMING OPPORTUNITIES

SHE WINS GLOBAL SUMMIT | LAS VEGAS | NOVEMBER 6–7, 2025
EMPOWERHER CONTENT DAY | LAS VEGAS | FEBRUARY 2026

SIGN UP TODAY

VISIT WWW.SHERISESSTUDIOS.COM/INTRODUCING-100-WOMEN-OF-IMPACT TO CLAIM YOUR SPOT.

![University of Leeds logo]

ENROLL FREE TODAY TO SCALE YOUR BUSINESS

She Rises Studios and Goldman Sachs 10,000 Women join forces to provide education, resources, and a supportive global community for women-led SMEs, empowering them to grow, innovate, and thrive in today's competitive landscape.

FROM PAIN TO POWER:

MY LIFE ON TWO WHEELS

By **Patty Mooney**

When I was 14, my left knee gave out while I was walking down the stairs at my high school. I collapsed in front of a crowd of students. The physical pain was intense, but the humiliation stung more. A doctor recommended surgery. He scraped away the remaining cartilage in my knee, a decision that would accelerate the degenerative arthritis already taking hold.

I limped through my teens and twenties, doing my best to live a normal life while pain quietly became my companion. What I didn't know then was that my path would one day lead to high mountain trails, to windswept ridges and rushing descents, to a life lived outdoors and in motion.

In 1986, I set out on a nine-month North American road trip with my partner, Mark Schulze. While browsing a sporting goods store in the Yukon, we noticed a neon-colored bicycle with fat knobby tires. *"It's called a mountain bike,"* the clerk told us. That moment lit a spark. When we returned to San Diego in time for Christmas, we gifted each other mountain bikes. That was the beginning of our mountain biking life.

The trails became my sanctuary. Riding turned out to be the best thing I could do for my knee. The circular motion strengthened the surrounding muscles and preserved what function remained. Mark and I combined our creative talents with our love of adventure and began producing the world's first instructional mountain biking videos. I not only co-produced the series and wrote the scripts, I also starred in three out of the four films. It was a groundbreaking experience that helped bring the sport to a wider audience. We also entered races and won. I felt strong, alive, and free.

But the damage was real. In my forties, the pain reached a tipping point. My knee x-rays were so severe that the orthopedic surgeon asked if he could use them in a PowerPoint presentation at a medical conference. I underwent my first Total Knee Replacement, a major surgery and a humbling reset. After a few years, my right knee began to deteriorate as well. Another surgery followed. Now I live with two titanium knees.

Some people assumed my biking days were over. They were not.

In 2023, at the age of 68, I entered the grueling 20-mile Sagebrush Safari mountain bike race. It is no gentle ride. It is a test of strength, endurance, and focus. I trained with care, listened to my body, and crossed the finish line first in my age group. In 2024, I returned and won again at age 69.

What does it mean to be unstoppable? When I was younger, I thought it meant forcing my way through everything. Now I know it means something else. It means respecting your body while refusing to be ruled by limitation. It means showing up, even when you're scared. It means allowing the pain to shape you, but never define you.

If I could speak to that 14-year-old girl who fell on the stairs, I would say, *"You are not broken. You are becoming. That pain you feel will become part of your story, but not the end of it. One day, you will ride through forests, across deserts, and up mountains. You will feel joy again, and you will triumph."*

Mountain biking didn't just give me strength. It gave me back my spirit. Every ride is a reminder that I didn't just survive. I soared.

And I'm still riding. Most days, I'm the only woman in a pack of male athletes, who look at me with amazement and respect. They've seen what I can do. And I'm just getting started.

Connect With Patty

www.pattymooney.com
www.facebook.com/patty.mooney1
www.instagram.com/pattymooney69

December 2025

FROM FEAR TO POWER:

MY THYROID CANCER STORY AND THE BIRTH OF A COMMUNITY

By **Isabel Márquez**
Co-founder of Thyroid Collective

The moment everything changed for me wasn't just when I was told I had thyroid cancer. It was the quiet after. The overwhelm. The disconnect. I felt like I had entered a version of life where no one quite knew how to meet me where I was, not even myself.

I was young and suddenly in a loop of appointments, scans, surgery, radioactive iodine treatment, and long silences. My body was doing one thing and my mind another. I felt fragile, but everyone around me thought I was being strong. I didn't want strength. I wanted clarity. I wanted someone to say, "*Me too.*"

As I started to recover physically, I realized something bigger. There was no real support for people like me. Yes, there was medical information out there, but it was often terrifying or too clinical. There was nothing that helped me understand what was happening to me as a whole person. Especially in Spanish. Especially as a Latina. Especially as someone who needed to feel like I still had agency over my life and body.

That realization turned into purpose. I co-founded Thyroid Collective to create what I needed but couldn't find: a digital community in Spanish, designed for people living with thyroid conditions to feel informed, guided, and seen.

Inside the community, we talk about the things that often go unsaid when you receive a diagnosis. How to make sense of lab results. How to talk to your doctor. What optimal treatment really looks like when you want more than "normal" labs. What foods support healing. What to ask in your first endocrinologist appointment. How to know if your supplements are working. We bring in experts in nutrition, functional medicine, gynecology, mental health, and more to lead real conversations. We ask the questions we wish someone had asked for us.

And yes, we also talk about the small things that matter more than people realize. Like which personal care products are non-toxic and safe for hormone-sensitive bodies. What exercise supports your energy instead of draining it. How to approach routines when your body feels unpredictable. How to feel like yourself again after surgery, treatment, or burnout.

For me, being unstoppable has changed. I used to think it meant pushing through everything and being productive no matter what. But in one of our planning sessions for an upcoming productivity talk, an expert said something that stayed with me. She said, *"In life, you can do everything. But you can't do everything at once. Find what season you're in— healing, building, creating—and make that your priority. Only then will you understand what productivity really is."*

That line shifted something in me. Being unstoppable isn't about being in motion. It's about being aligned. It's choosing what matters right now and giving yourself fully to it. It's knowing when to pause and when to move. When to lead and when to listen. And it's using what you've lived through to help someone else feel less alone in what they're living now.

If I could speak to the version of myself who almost gave up, I'd tell her this:

You are not too much
You are not too late

You are not broken
You are becoming

The pain will pass but the clarity it gives you will stay. And one day, this thing that nearly crushed you will become the exact thing that connects you to hundreds of others. That's what Thyroid Collective has become. And it's just the beginning.

Connect With Isabel

www.instagram.com/thyroidcollective_
www.tiktok.com/@isabelpmp

THE SUBCONSCIOUS SHIFTS THAT CHANGED MY LIFE

By **Faye Casement**
Certified Professional Life Coach, Subconscious Belief Facilitator, and Reiki Master
Founder of Reflect, Grow and Heal

For a long time, I didn't realise I was carrying emotional weight. I just thought I was doing what everyone else did, getting on with it. That heaviness would show through in my energy, my mood, my physical health and my sense of self. I felt sluggish in every sense. Tired, drained, and disconnected from who I was.

I ticked all the boxes: education, marriage, baby, career. On the surface, I looked successful. But inside, I felt numb and lost. I wasn't choosing my life. I was following the script, playing all the roles, and wearing all the masks. The good girl. The hard worker. The people-pleaser. The superhero.

I spent the first 40 years of my life living from fear, not freedom. Fear of being seen. Fear of getting it wrong. Fear that if I stopped performing or proving my worth, I'd be judged and let people down.

The wounds began early. Playground name-calling planted the seeds of shame. My sensitivity made me feel like I didn't belong. I learned to blend in, to perform, to suppress who I really was. Beneath all of it was a relentless belief, sometimes quiet, sometimes loud, that I wasn't enough.

By my teens, that belief had taken over. Crippling low self-esteem led to poor choices, emotional shutdown, and long periods of darkness. There were times I truly didn't want to be here, and those years were filled with invisible pain and deep inner disconnection.

Everything began to shift when I discovered life coaching. For the first time, someone helped me see I wasn't broken. I was carrying beliefs and emotional weight that weren't mine to hold. I learned I could let them go. That I got to choose. That I could move from passenger to creator in my own life.

That spark led me into deeper emotional and spiritual healing. I trained in subconscious belief work. I discovered how the body stores what the mind can't process, and how much power we reclaim when we gently go there. I became a Reiki Master. I unlearned, I grieved, I grew, and slowly, I came home to myself.

The woman I am today isn't perfect. But she's powerful. She knows who she is. And on the days she forgets, she knows how to come back to who she is. I don't just talk about having a toolbox. I genuinely have one now, filled with practices that meet me where I am.

A few years ago, I chose the word unstoppable as my guiding intention. It doesn't mean I never wobble. It means I no longer abandon myself when I do. It means I don't believe the old story that I can't do anything about it. I trust myself now. I know how to reset when life gets heavy.

Today, I work as an Energy and Emotional Reset Facilitator. I help others shift the beliefs, energy, and emotional patterns that are weighing them down so they can reconnect with their own clarity, spark, and sense of self. The biggest subconscious shifts I've made, and now support others with, are the beliefs that say: I shouldn't be seen. I'm not enough. I don't matter. These old stories once ran the show. Now, they've been replaced with trust, worth, and self-leadership.

Becoming unstoppable is not about doing more. It's about releasing what holds us back and reclaiming our truth.

Life has been a rollercoaster, but it was never the end of the story. And the beautiful part is, we always get to rewrite it if we're willing and with the right support.

Connect With Faye

www.reflectgrowandheal.com
Instagram: @reflectgrowandheal
Facebook: fayecasement3a

she wins
WOMEN'S NETWORK

Elevate your business with the power of community.

Get access to the tools, connections, and support you need to grow—with a circle of women who truly get it.

WHAT'S INCLUDED

- Strategic networking & mentorship
- Expert-led masterclasses & exclusive resources
- Member spotlights, VIP perks & more

Join for just

$87/MONTH

no contracts, cancel anytime.

www.shewinswomensnetwork.com

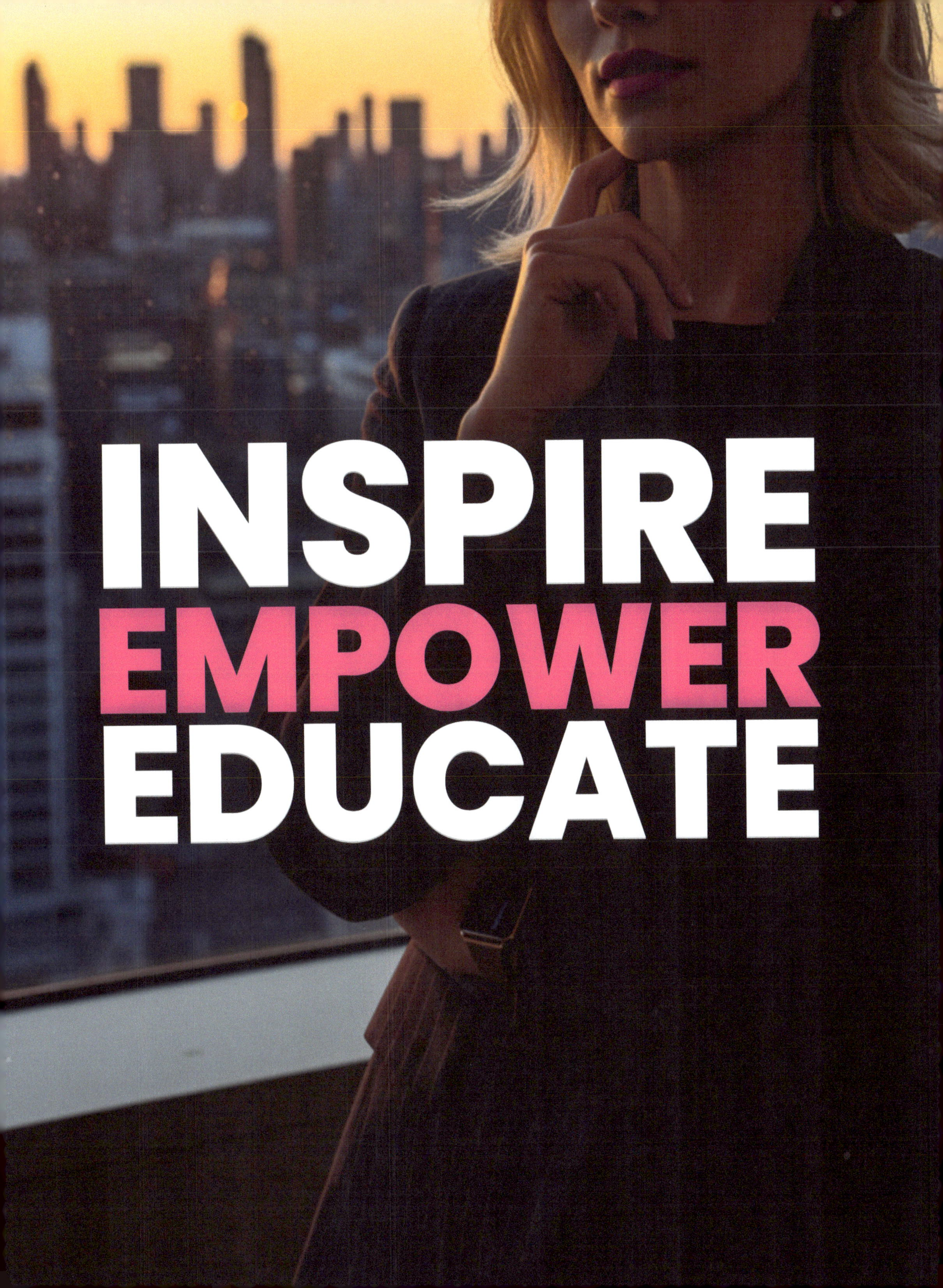
INSPIRE
EMPOWER
EDUCATE

THE NIGHT I REALISED RESILIENCE ISN'T QUIET OR HIDDEN

By **Katie Lynch**

Sometimes it looks like laughter, confetti, and the courage to start again.

When I threw my divorce party over ten years ago, people thought I was joking. Divorce wasn't something you celebrated. It was supposed to be sad, heavy, even shameful. But I had carried enough of that. I wanted to rewrite the story.

People probably expected tears or bitterness. What they didn't expect was me in a cheeky outfit, swinging at a giant penis piñata in the garage while my friends cheered. It wasn't about shock value. It was about reclaiming joy and proving to myself that I could turn heartbreak into something light, funny, and unforgettable.

Early into our relationship, I gave up a career I loved to provide us with stability. It was only me and him then, but the dream was to create a family and a life together. When the marriage fell apart, it felt like everything I had invested in was gone. That family dream went, but the kids and all of our things remained.

That night in the garage reminded me I still had the power to shape my own story. Resilience didn't need to be quiet or hidden. It could be loud, playful, even a little outrageous. What mattered was that it came from a place of courage, the courage to let go of shame and step into a new chapter with laughter instead of regret.

Over time, that moment became more than just a funny memory. It was proof that I could face challenges head-on and still choose joy. Life since then hasn't been easy or perfect. I've been through another divorce, am raising independent kids with the support of family, friends and my second husband, and started building a business when it might have been easier to give up. I am the family's circus ring leader, the one managing it all, juggling the chaos and keeping the show moving forward.

That spark of courage became the foundation for what I built next. In the same year, I started my business from home with a small printer so I could be there for my kids. The career I once loved and studied so hard to get into, the one I gave up for a stable family life, I got back in my own way. This time, it was mine. I built something that gave me freedom, creativity, and the ability to create magical memories for my children while also helping thousands of other families celebrate their milestones.

I also began to see resilience in a different light. For me, it wasn't about keeping quiet, pushing through without emotion, or pretending everything was fine. Resilience was about finding healthy ways to move forward, even if that meant being a little outrageous. Smashing a piñata might not be the traditional picture of strength, but for me, it was a turning point.

There is still stigma around divorce, and I feel it even more now than I did back then. When I tell people I'm divorced, let alone twice, I see their reactions. When I say I'm a single mum, I know what some people assume. But these labels don't make me less of a person. If anything, they show my strength. They prove that I was willing to keep going, to protect my kids, and to carve out a life for us even when the path was difficult.

What people don't often talk about is how much creativity and even catharsis can come from those hard times. Planning that party gave me something to look forward to. It distracted me from the endless cycle of grief, the reliving of happy and painful memories, and the dreams that had been shattered. I won't pretend I didn't grieve. I cried plenty, and I think that's healthy. It is important to feel those emotions and let them out. But after a couple of months, it was time to move forward, and I wanted to do it with my head held high.

That night taught me that resilience can be joyful. It can be bold. It can even be silly. And that perspective carried into my business too. Every time I create something bright, fun, and personal for a customer's celebration, I'm reminded that joy is worth fighting for.

Resilience doesn't always look like silence, strength, or pushing through quietly. Sometimes it looks like laughter echoing from the garage, confetti on the floor, and a woman with a stick in her hand taking one last swing at the past before stepping into the future.

Connect With Katie

www.linkedin.com/in/katie-lynch-0a191b1b3
www.facebook.com/KatieJDesignAndEvents
www.instagram.com/katiejdesignandevents
www.au.pinterest.com/KatieJEvents
www.tiktok.com/@katiejdesignandevents

© JESS MCGILLICUDDY PHOTOGRAPHY

PALM CLUB
DESIGN GROUP:

DESIGN INSPIRED RENOVATION EXPERTS

By **Kiersten Miller**

I have never thought of myself as particularly bold. Growing up in Cape Town, South Africa, I poured my energy into a coffee roastery I owned in the middle of a lively design district. Every day I was surrounded by artists, furniture makers, and craftspeople. Watching them work taught me that true beauty lies in craftsmanship and in the care someone puts into what they create. Even though I loved being part of that community, my appreciation for design stayed quietly in the background of my life. When my husband, John, and I moved to New York in 2018 for his work, I started importing artisan pieces from South Africa.

They were textiles, ceramics, and sculptures that told a story of culture and tradition. The business itself was not a runaway success, but it refined my eye and reminded me of how much I wanted design to be part of my future. I realized I did not just want to curate. I wanted to create. Then the pandemic came, and everything changed. Suddenly, the world slowed down and homes became the center of our lives. In the middle of all that uncertainty, we made the decision to move to Florida with our daughter, Neave. At the time it felt like a leap into the unknown, but it was also the most courageous decision I had ever made.

That move changed everything. Soon after we arrived, we reconnected with new friends, Jon and Taylor Scurry, who were in the middle of a home renovation. We began helping them and, little by little, what started as a neighborly gesture grew into a collaboration. Jon's design eye blended with John's systems mindset, and I found myself weaving in my global sensibility and attention to detail. Together we realized we could do something bigger than just help friends renovate. We could create a firm that guided people through every step of transforming their homes. That is how Palm Club Design Group was born. We are not simply interior designers. We are partners for the entire renovation process, from the very first idea to the final finishing touches. Our work is about transformation and trust, and about creating homes that feel both personal and elevated. Today we proudly call ourselves Design Inspired Renovation Experts. Looking back, I see that moving to Florida was not just about location. It was about courage.

It was about believing that instincts I had carried with me since those early days in Cape Town could guide us toward something meaningful. That leap gave me the chance to build a business, a team, and a community centered on creating homes that reflect who people truly are. For me, courage looked like leaving behind the familiar and stepping into a space where creativity and trust could shape something new. It changed not just my career but my life.

Connect With Kiersten

www.palmclubdesigngroup.com

© JESS MCGILLICUDDY PHOTOGRAPHY

RECOMMENDED BY
DERMATOLOGISTS

BEFORE   AFTER

THE ORIGINAL
WRINKLE FREE
STRAW

REUSABLE

2 Inch

SIPFACE
Anti-Aging
STRAWS
Set of 2

NOT JUST ANTI-AGING

SipFace
WRINKLE FREE
STRAWS

Healthy Sipping Starts Here

Hot & cold drink compatible

Eco-friendly and durable

BPA-free, food-grade

WWW.SIPFACESTRAW.COM

RIDING THE WAVES:

MY JOURNEY TO OWNING MY POWER

By **Bridget Sorenson**

If you told me 15 years ago that I would one day run a thriving networking organization, mentor leaders, and watch 6-figure deals spark from introductions I facilitated, I wouldn't have believed you. Before I got divorced I was a busy mother, with five children in five different schools, working a minimum-wage job. *"Owning my power"* wasn't even in my vocabulary. Survival was.

My first turning point came when I realized that minimum wage wasn't going to sustain my family after divorce. I pivoted into financial services, where I organized *"lunch and learn"* sessions for law firms and built relationships with professionals across industries. It was in those rooms that I discovered something important: I had a gift for connecting people—not just in casual conversation, but in ways that led to opportunities and lasting partnerships.

One lawyer friend noticed it, too. He told me, *"You have a way of bringing the right people into the same room. You should build a business around that."* Together, we drafted the blueprint for what would later become my company, Blue Water Wave—a community for vetted professionals focused on excellence, integrity, and superior client relationships. But at the time, financial services was my main income, and my new venture was only a side passion.

Then came the second turning point, one that would change my life in every way. I was preparing for a major accreditation exam required to advance my financial services career. In that industry, you also have to regularly retake certifications—my next one was due in May 2021. Just before exam weekend, I found a lump in my breast. By Thursday, I had my diagnosis: breast cancer. By Tuesday, I was in surgery.

In that moment, my plans came to a screeching halt. If I didn't take the test that weekend, I would have to start over in financial services. But something deep inside told me to let it go. My health came first. I chose surgery, recovery, and life over a test.

That choice, though terrifying, freed me. I stopped clinging to the security of my financial services career and turned my full focus to Blue Water Wave. While recovering from cancer, I poured myself into building it. Within a year, my business tripled.

Blue Water Wave is now a thriving networking organization that helps leaders grow through organic marketing, LinkedIn strategy, and curated connections—whether on the golf course, over Zoom, or in person. We host events where real business happens, but more importantly, we nurture trust. We vet every member, ensuring their business reflects excellence and integrity. I work one-on-one with members to help them become thought leaders and achieve ROI on their relationships.

My leadership style has been shaped by both the calm and the storms of my life. Yoga and Taoist teachings taught me to let go and flow with the current, rather than fight against it. I've learned that life will hand you unexpected waves—divorce, cancer, career shifts—and the key is knowing when to paddle hard and when to trust the tide to carry you.

Today, I see myself as the captain of a ship powered by the collective ambition of my members. When they ask for new chapters—a women's group, a young professionals circle—I create them. I mentor emerging leaders, sharing my story so they understand: your power is not in controlling every twist in the current. It's in knowing you can navigate no matter where it takes you.

Owning my power wasn't about charging ahead without fear—it was about faith and recognizing my resilience, leaning into my gift for connecting people, and trusting the waves that life put in front of me. Looking back, I see that every pivot, every surrender, and every moment of uncertainty was guiding me toward exactly where I was meant to be–and owning my power!

About Bridget Sorenson

Bridget Sorenson is the CEO of Blue Water Wave (BWW), an exclusive networking organization that does organic marketing for its members. With over two decades of experience in digital and events marketing, Bridget's career spans financial services, commercial real estate, and C-Level consulting. She has worked for and with Fortune 100 & 500 companies, as well as leading brands such as Louis Vuitton, Ralph Lauren, Chanel, and Northwestern Mutual. At the helm at BWW, Bridget bridges her business acumen with being *"the wave,"* as those closest to her deemed her, attributed to her keen sense of connecting professionals to drive their success. Follow her on LinkedIn.

Connect With Bridget

www.bluewaterwave.com
www.linkedin.com/in/bridget-l-sorenson-bluewaterwave

FROM "STUPID GIRL" TO SYSTEM-BREAKER

By **Britt Bischoff**

I didn't grow up believing I was destined for much. Born to a teenage mother and raised around abusive father figures, I spent my early years hearing that I was "*stupid*" and would never amount to anything. I became quiet, afraid to speak up, and accustomed to shrinking myself so I wouldn't be judged.

My stepfather's words echoed in my mind: "*You'll never amount to anything.*" It was with an "*I'll show you*" attitude that I put myself through college, self-paid, becoming the first in my family to graduate and earn a college degree. But even then, I was living as half of myself.

A defining moment came on New Year's Eve 2014. I set an intention to become fearless, to create a life I could be proud of, to touch lives, to explore, and to let my humanitarian heart shine without fear. I didn't know the exact path, but I knew I couldn't continue hiding anymore.

In the years that followed, I said "*yes*" to the unknown. I traveled the country alone with my dog, climbing mountains and finding myself in moments that tested my courage. My car's brakes failed in Yosemite. I stared down a mountain lion. I survived a bullet through my apartment wall. That's just the tip of the iceberg.

Life has challenged me. Each challenge proved I was stronger and more capable than I'd been told. More importantly, each experience taught me to trust my own voice, my own instincts.

Fearlessness became my compass. I embraced new careers, new experiences, new opportunities, new locations. I became a nomad, eventually moving across the country. Each struggle taught me about my own resilience. Each risk revealed more of who I really was.

I began listening to myself - my inner thoughts, my own creativity. I learned to sit alone with myself and trust what I heard. This was revolutionary for someone who'd spent years believing others knew better than I did about my own capabilities.

Professionally, this meant walking away from a well-paying leadership role to stand up to toxic bosses and workplace bullies. It meant standing on my own, building my own consulting business from the ground up. It meant taking the risk to create an entirely new AI tool. The struggles that followed forced me to finally recognize how smart I actually am. (Smart enough that several industry & tech leaders have siphoned my work.) I developed award-winning frameworks that help campaigns and organizations disrupt digital manipulation, creating new approaches to political strategy that challenge the status quo.

Today, I lead my own business and have become a recognized voice in this space. My multi-award-winning strategies have helped pass ballot initiatives protecting reproductive rights across multiple states. I've exposed state-based propaganda campaigns, defended vulnerable communities from targeted digital attacks, and trained national networks to fight coordinated narrative attacks. The quiet girl became the loud advocate.

I stand on my own because I know who I am. I face hard challenges because I believe deeply in myself and refuse to let the world tell me what I'm capable of.

The girl who was called "*stupid*" now leads strategy that disrupts entrenched power and protects freedoms.

I'm no longer the girl who couldn't speak up for herself. I am the badass my younger self needed. I take up space, refuse to accept "*that's just the way it is,*" and create change for those who come after me.

Only time will tell if I've stepped completely into my full power. My life today is unrecognizable from where I began, and I'm just getting started.

Connect With Britt

britt@brittbischoff.com
www.brittannica.substack.com
www.brittbischoff.com
www.linkedin.com/in/brittbischoff
www.x.com/BrittBischoff

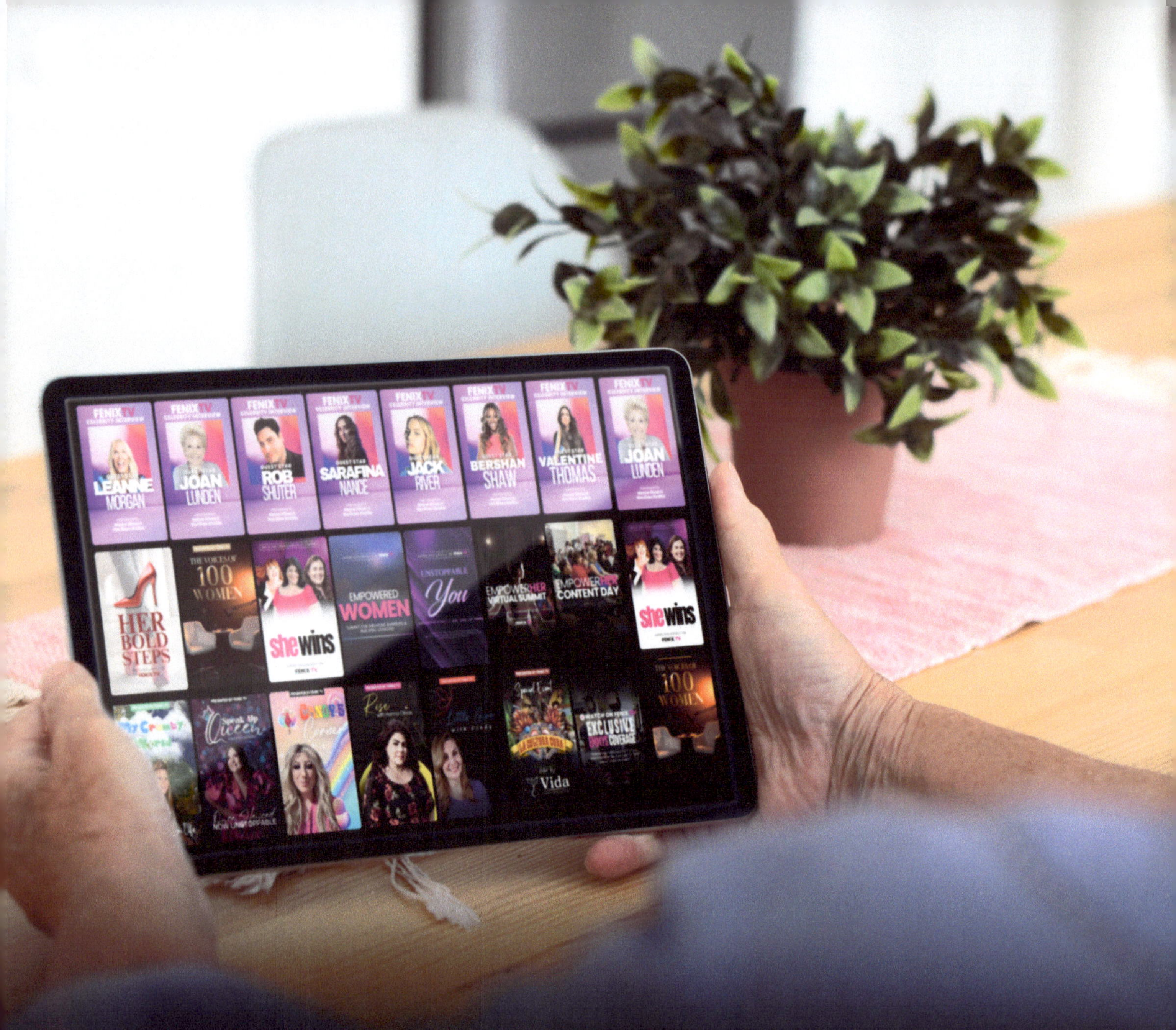

A NEW CHAPTER BEGINS

FENIX TV

IS NOW ON YOUTUBE

TUNE IN FOR THE SAME INSPIRING CONTENT YOU LOVE, NOW ON A GLOBAL STAGE.

SHOP NOW

GRAB YOUR COPY NOW

Possibility to Prosperity is an inspiring anthology featuring bold, visionary women who turned their greatest struggles into triumphs. Through honest and powerful stories, these women reveal how pain can become purpose, fear can become fuel, and setbacks can spark success. From heartbreak and burnout to rejection and failure, each chapter offers lessons in resilience, reinvention, and reclaiming one's worth. With courage and determination, these stories illuminate the path from challenge to opportunity, showing that it's never too late to rise, build, and thrive. This book reminds every reader that your struggles can be the gateway to your greatest possibilities.

amazon.com   SHE RISES STUDIOS

THE POWER FOUND IN THE SPACE BETWEEN CRISIS & GROWTH

By **Kristin-Marie Pernicano**

3

I used to think owning my power meant having control over everything. I was wrong.

Two and a half years ago, my life unexpectedly shifted. I discovered I had a rare, aggressive, stage 3 breast cancer related to 9/11. I was forced to become something I'd never prepared for: simultaneously being a full-time patient, practitioner, and professor.

The irony wasn't lost on me. I'd spent 15+ years building operational frameworks for other people's businesses, but I had no systems for my own life when the worst possible crisis hit.

During my first intensive chemo treatment, facing a seven-year journey, I made myself a promise: If I survived, I would finally build the digital ecosystem I'd been talking about forever, but had been too afraid to create.

For ten years, I'd discussed launching the Business Decoded Series but found excuses. Building other companies from concepts to seven-figure brands felt easier than believing in myself. I could transform others into leaders but froze when investing more in myself.

The patterns were clear: I was brilliant at seeing potential in everyone except the person in the mirror.

Cancer didn't make me stronger. It revealed who I already was. Unlike the highly overused platitude, cancer didn't create anything new in me. It stripped away everything I was hiding behind and forced me to stop living small while helping others live large.

I'd always said yes to things that scared me, except fully believing in myself. Goldman Sachs as a liberal arts major? Yes. Teaching despite public speaking fear? Yes. Building others' seven-figure companies? Absolutely. But creating my own platform? Too exposed.

During treatment, I was hustling with energy I didn't have, dragging myself to campus twice a week while surviving chemo, surgeries, reconstruction, immunotherapy, and radiation.

It was my worst nightmare: performing for everyone while my body fought for its life. I was jealous of those who could afford to just be patients.

But in that impossible space, I finally understood the cost of not building systems for myself. How many opportunities had I missed being more comfortable helping others than investing in my own vision?

I wasn't becoming someone new...I was finally stepping into who I'd always been. The revelation wasn't about learning new definitions of power; I'd been teaching those for years. It was about applying them to myself instead of just to others.

I used to think owning my power meant being indispensable to everyone else's success while staying invisible. Now I know it means being willing to be seen, to bet on my vision with the same confidence I've always had in others.

Three Things I Learned About My Own Power

1. I was saying yes to everything that scared me except betting on myself. I could transform others because the risk felt manageable. But my own goals felt too daunting.
2. My patterns revealed my power. I was doing effortlessly for others what I resisted doing for myself. The same skills that made me indispensable to their success could make me unstoppable for my own.
3. I was compounding missed opportunities. Every time I chose others' comfort over my growth, I trained myself to stay small. But betting on myself builds the muscle for greater impact.

Your power isn't something you find. It's something you build, one framework at a time, one moment of choosing growth over comfort at a time.

Advice for my former self? Stop hiding your brilliance behind other people's success. The world doesn't need another person making everyone else look good from the shadows. It needs you- fully visible, unapologetically brilliant, and finally willing to bet on yourself.

Connect With Kristin-Marie

www.linkedin.com/in/kristinmariepernicano
www.kmp-consulting.com/
www.instagram.com/kmp.consulting

CONFIDENCE ISN'T BORN, IT'S BUILT

By **Marci Hopkins**

The alarm went off. It was a Monday, the start of a new week. Before I even opened my eyes, the anxiety crept in. The pressure to be everything to everyone else. The guilt of not doing enough. And the fog from the wine I'd used the night before to *"cope."*

That was my life almost ten years ago: exhausted, overwhelmed, and silently drowning. On the outside, I looked like I had it together. On the inside, I was falling apart.

What changed everything for me wasn't just getting sober, it was learning to reconnect with myself and to build my confidence from the inside out. I realized I had been living for everyone else's approval, measuring my worth by achievements, perfection, and people-pleasing. But real transformation began the moment I gave myself **permission...**permission to not be perfect, to ask for help, and to finally put myself first.

That permission was the spark that lit the fire of confidence within me.

Confidence Isn't Born, It's Built

Confidence isn't about walking into a room and being the loudest voice. It's about walking into a room knowing you are enough, whether anyone notices or not. For me, confidence was built one small choice at a time.
- Choosing gratitude instead of guilt.
- Choosing boundaries instead of burnout.
- Choosing forgiveness instead of shame.

Each choice was a brick in the foundation of a new life...one rooted in peace, clarity, and joy.

As I grew in confidence, doors began to open. I became the host of *Wake Up with Marci*, an inspirational television show on CBS WLNY-TV. I launched my podcast to dive deeper into meaningful conversations around healing and mental health. I wrote my award-winning book, *Chaos to Clarity*. I am a motivational speaker, and I have built a life changing program, *Chaos to Clarity: From Stuck to Thriving*, to guide other women through the same transformation.

None of this happened overnight. But it all started with one decision: to believe I was worthy of change.

Why Confidence Creates Change

Confidence is contagious. When you find your voice, you give others permission to find theirs too.

When you stop apologizing for your worth, you model for your children, your colleagues, and your community what it looks like to own your power.

That's why I speak openly about my healing journey because confidence grows when we strip away shame and speak our truths. I want women to know: you don't have to earn your worth. You already have it.

How You Can Start Today

If you're reading this and wondering how to begin, let me offer three simple steps:
- **Gratitude First** – Each morning, write down three things you're grateful for. Gratitude rewires your brain to see what you have instead of what's missing.
- **One Boundary** – Say no to one thing this week that drains you. Notice how much energy it frees up.
- **Forgive Yourself** – Write a letter to yourself releasing the guilt of one past mistake. Remind yourself: you did the best you could with what you knew at the time.

These practices may seem small, but they're powerful. They help shift your mindset from powerless to empowered, from stuck to thriving.

My Call to You

Confidence isn't about changing who you are, it's about returning to who you've always been. Underneath the guilt, the shame, and the fear, your worth has never left you.
So today, I want to leave you with this truth:
- You deserve a life of gratitude.
- You deserve a life of confidence.
- You deserve a life of joy.

Let this be your permission: To rise. To thrive. To wake up to your worth.

Connect With Marci

www.wakeupwithmarci.com
www.instagram.com/wake_up_with_marci
www.youtube.com/channel/UCtv2M6RTE
YmUkLnkGgcg7Rw

SHE RISES STUDIOS

Live Tour

10 CITIES. 2 WEEKS. EMPOWERING WOMEN EVERYWHERE.

JANUARY **12-26**   REGISTER NOW

EMPOWERHER CONTENT DAY

ONE STADIUM. 40,000 WOMEN. INFINITE IMPACT

02 | 22 | 2026

FINDING ME

By **Tara Gordon**

Three weeks before my picture-perfect New York City wedding, I walked away. I quit my corporate job, sold my apartment, and booked a one-way ticket to Tel Aviv. On paper, it looked reckless. In reality, it was the first time I'd ever truly chosen myself.

I grew up in the 80s and 90s with every privilege you could ask for—good schools, the right sports, the right camps, a neatly mapped-out path. But privilege came with strings and expectations. I followed the plan, yet I never really fit in.

In my 20s, I was a corporate recruiter and I co-founded a nonprofit I believed in with all my heart. The mission mattered, but the work rarely played to my strengths.

My father and brother thrived in business; my mother quietly powered our family from behind the scenes. I admired all of them, but I wanted something entirely my own—where I could be both the visionary and the engine.

It wasn't until those months abroad, wandering and thinking, that I realized there's a difference between going through life and truly living it. When I came home, I decided—almost on a whim—to get certified as a Pilates instructor. I thought it would be a side gig while I wrote a book. Instead, it became my calling.

Teaching Pilates awakened a confidence I hadn't felt before.

I discovered my gift for helping people reconnect with their bodies and their strength. The work was tangible, immediate, and deeply fulfilling. After several years of teaching, I opened my first studio, 212 Pilates, in New York City.

Today, 212 Pilates is a thriving, spine-safe community where we keep group reformer classes small and offer accessible options for clients with back pain, osteoporosis, or pre/postnatal needs—without requiring them to disclose personal health details. We've expanded into a beautiful, larger space, built a loyal client base, and created a place where people feel truly seen.

Now, I get to guide new instructors through a certification program that didn't exist when I started—mentoring them on a path that changed my life.

What began as a *"maybe"* has grown into a career, a community, and a legacy.

My journey taught me this: the most powerful chapters often start when you step off the path you thought you were meant to follow.

Connect With Tara

Instagram: @_taragordon @212pilatesstudio
TikTok: tara_gordon 212pilates

MORE WORKOUT, LESS TIME!

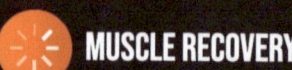 **MUSCLE RECOVERY**   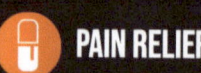 **PAIN RELIEF**    **STRESS REDUCTION**    **WEIGHT LOSS**

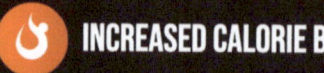 **INCREASED CALORIE BURN**    **DETOXIFICATION**    **LOWER BLOOD PRESSURE**

 CELLULITE REDUCTION   **ANTI-AGING & SKIN REJUVENATION**   **IMPROVED CIRCULATION**

HOTWORX®
24 HOUR INFRARED FITNESS STUDIO

PACK RIGHT
TRAVEL LIGHT

Look and Feel Your Best on Any Adventure!

SHOP NOW
YUDIVABEAUTY.COM

FROM BURNOUT TO BELIEF:

THE JOURNEY THAT CREATED THE THOUGHTFUL LEADER

By **Jill Golledge**

Growing up, I was always one of the quieter ones, constantly told to *"speak up more"* or *"contribute more in group discussions."* I rarely put my hand up to answer questions in class and I hated the thought of standing in front of others to speak. The burning cheeks, sweaty palms, and racing heartbeat became too familiar. Then, I didn't understand these physical reactions, I just thought something was wrong with me. Fifteen years would pass before I discovered I was an introvert, suddenly, everything made sense.

It was in my mid-twenties that I first completed the Myers-Briggs personality test and realised the word introvert applied to me. It explained why I struggled with decision-making, especially about my own life; why I disliked small talk and found conversations with strangers so draining.

Back then, I hadn't realised the strengths my introversion gave me. My natural tendency to look for innovative solutions instead of complaining was a hidden asset. My ability to focus and attention to detail were exactly the qualities that had allowed me to excel in forensic science. Unfortunately, for many years, I'd been focused on what I lacked rather than the skills I possessed.

I spent over twenty-five years working in a large organisation, navigating the unique challenges introverts face in workplaces designed for extroverts. Open-plan offices drained me, meetings made it difficult for my voice to be heard, and I struggled to secure that promotion. Truthfully, I held myself back from pursuing senior leadership roles, not because I lacked ability, but because I doubted myself and worried about being judged.

By the end of 2021, I reached burnout. Covid-19 hit, and I was wearing many hats: forensic scientist, coach, home-school teacher, wife, daughter, and mother. The workload was relentless, and like many introverts, I placed everyone else's needs above my own. Perfectionism kept me striving, but the pressure became impossible to sustain.

When I finally asked for help, I didn't get the support I needed from my manager, so I created my own strategies. I set firmer boundaries, stopped taking on more than I could handle, and focused on one small task at a time.

I carved out self-care moments and sought coaching, which gave me the clarity I had been searching for: I didn't just need to recover, I needed to change direction completely.

That realisation began my transformation. I asked myself: What really matters to me? The answer became clear, helping others develop, grow, and become their best selves. That's when I decided to step into my own self-belief and start my business. The Thoughtful Leader was born.

Becoming an entrepreneur demanded a massive mindset shift. I had to move from seeing myself as just an employee to embracing the identity of a business owner. I had to believe that I could make it happen, even though it had never been a dream. Sharing my voice and my perspective felt uncomfortable at first, but I reminded myself of something powerful: when I am passionate about fairness and justice, I always find my voice.

Today, I no longer hide behind self-doubt. I know, without question, that introverts make incredible leaders. We bring thoughtfulness, depth, innovation, and authenticity into spaces that desperately need it. My mission is to ensure other introverts don't shrink themselves to fit into an extroverted mould. Instead, I help them embrace their unique strengths and step into leadership with confidence, passion, and authenticity.

Starting my business wasn't just about creating a new career, it was about stepping into my own self-belief for the first time. And once I did that, everything changed.

Connect With Jill

www.thethoughtfulleader.global
www.linkedin.com/in/jill-golledge
Instagram: @the.thoughtful.leader
www.instagram.com/the.thoughtful.leader
www.youtube.com/@thethoughtfulleader
www.facebook.com/groups/introvertedambitiouswomen
www.tiktok.com/thethoughtfulleader

THE RISE OF A NEW KIND OF WOMAN:

HOW THE CELLARA METHOD IS REDEFINING STRENGTH, LEADERSHIP, AND LEGACY

By **She Rises Studios Editorial Team**

Heather Hanson has spent nearly three decades reshaping how high achievers think about wellness. Where many programs promise one more protocol, one more productivity hack, Hanson offers a different map. Her work centers on safety, nervous system regulation, and a radical return to self. Known as a calm, authoritative guide, she teaches women to move from survival into strength. Her Cellara Method blends physiology, neuroscience, and spiritual practice into a pathway that restores energy, clarity, and a steady sense of purpose.

Her creation, The Cellara Method, emerged from her own story of being the woman who did everything right and still became sick, the woman who achieved success while suppressing emotion, and the woman who believed rest was something to be earned only after perfection. Life shattered that belief through betrayal, burnout, rebuilding her business from the ground up, and the devastating loss of her son. In those moments, she learned the truth that would become the foundation of her work. The nervous system tells the truth long before the mind is willing to admit it.

Cellara is not a symptom management tool. It is a framework for releasing survival patterns, restoring regulation, and reimagining life from within.

For her, the legacy she is building with this work reaches far beyond hormones, trauma, gut health, or embodiment. Those are simply the doorways. The real legacy is teaching women to stop abandoning themselves in the name of achievement and to redefine what power looks like for future generations. She imagines a world where women lead without self-betrayal, age with authority rather than fear, treat peace as a baseline instead of a reward, and define success by alignment rather than performance.

She has spent years reminding women that rising harder is not the answer. Cellara exists to teach women how to rise softer. And when a woman returns to safety in her own body, she becomes a different kind of leader. She shifts from reactive to grounded, from overwhelmed to intuitive, from self-sacrificing to self-honoring, from masked to powerful in her authenticity. This kind of woman influences generations.

Her professional philosophy was shaped not by a single moment but by many. However, there was one moment that transformed everything. For most of her life, she believed survival was strength. She had overcome autoimmunity, childhood trauma, betrayal, burnout, and rebuilding her career. She wore her resilience like armor. But when her son passed away, nothing she knew about discipline, nutrition, or strategy could protect her from grief. While navigating that loss, she fell back into familiar patterns of holding everything together for everyone else, suppressing her emotions to function, and disconnecting from her body to keep moving. That was when she realized she was not healing. She was performing strength.

In the quietest moments of her grief, something shifted. Her body asked to lead. Not with positivity, effort, or performance, but with presence. That shift revealed a truth she now teaches thousands: survival braces, but strength belongs to itself. This insight shaped the three pillars that define the Cellara framework. Release the patterns and emotions that keep a woman trapped in survival. Restore safety, nourishment, and regulation in the nervous system. Reimagine identity, purpose, and leadership from a grounded, embodied state.

Science supports her work, but the moment that initiated it was not scientific. It was sacred. She learned that the nervous system does not heal because we push harder. It heals when we become safe enough to feel.

Her work also exposes the hidden cost of over-functioning. Many women believe the cost is exhaustion. She believes the real cost is self-abandonment. In over-functioning, women become productive rather than present, responsible rather than resourced, and impressive rather than embodied. They tolerate draining relationships, take on roles no one asked them to hold, silence themselves to keep the peace, and diminish their brilliance to be palatable. The world still gets them, but they no longer get themselves.

She teaches that women do not burn out because they lack strength. They burn out because they remain strong for too long without support. So the first bold step toward freedom is simple. Let someone support you before you think you deserve it. When a woman receives support, her nervous system no longer has to choose between survival and success. Boundaries sharpen. Intuition strengthens. Leadership becomes compassionate rather than costly. She becomes undeniable.

Her clients describe her work as a return to self. In a world that constantly pulls women outward, she teaches them to live from the inside out. When a woman comes home to herself, her choices come from alignment, not obligation. Her boundaries rise from self-respect, not fear. Her rest becomes intentional, not earned. Her leadership flows from embodiment rather than performance. A woman who is home in herself does not dominate rooms. She transforms them.

As she reflects on her own legacy, her hope is simple yet powerful. She wants women to rise without depletion, lead without self-abandonment, and leave a mark without disappearing. She believes women are already strong. Her work exists to help them become strong and supported, powerful and peaceful, ambitious and regulated. She hopes future generations grow up knowing that rest is wisdom, emotion is safe, support is strength, peace is power, and worth is inherent.

If her life and her pain can show even one girl that she never has to choose between success and peace, then her legacy has already begun.

Connect With Heather

www.instagram.com/flourishnutritionaltherapy
www.facebook.com/heather.hanson.7773
www.facebook.com/flourishntp
www.linkedin.com/in/heather-hanson-870752b1
www.flourishnutritionaltherapy.com

SHOP NOW

GRAB YOUR COPY NOW

She Endures: Perseverance Through Pain is a heartfelt anthology honoring women who have faced life's hardest moments and chosen to rise. Through honest, powerful stories of illness, loss, heartbreak, and healing, this collection reveals how pain can shape strength and purpose. Each chapter offers hope, reminding readers that endurance is not just surviving, but growing through what we overcome. Featuring Hanna Olivas, Adriana Luna Carlos, and 11 inspiring authors, this book is a testament to the resilience of women who refuse to give up.

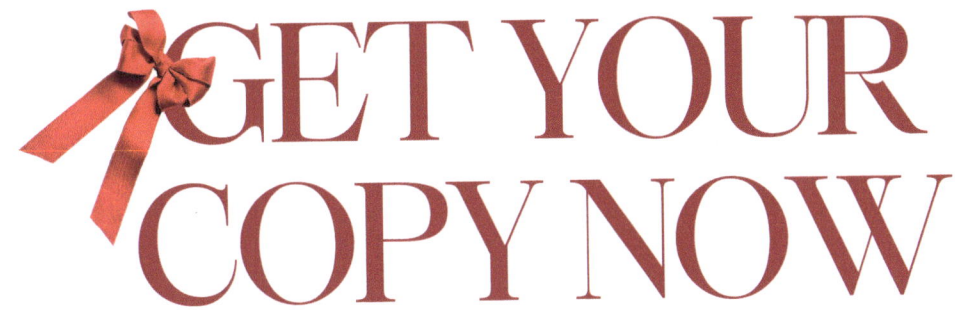

GET YOUR COPY NOW

Celebrate the power of women through inspiring stories and insights.

FAITH, FREEDOM & OTHER F WORDS
RHIANNON ANDERSON

THE ABCS OF SELF-LOVE
AMIE RICH

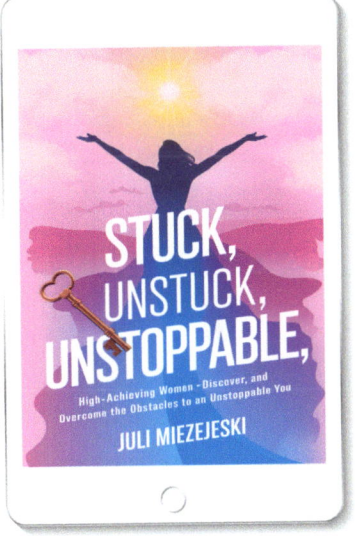

STUCK, UNSTUCK, UNSTOPPABLE
JULIA MIEZEJESKI

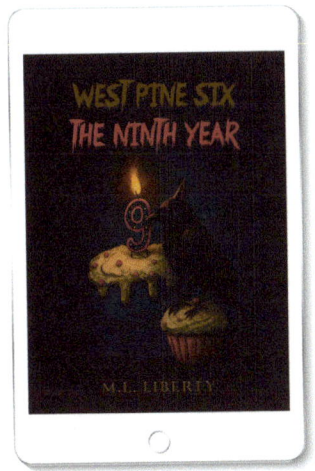

WEST PINE SIX: THE NINTH YEAR
MARIE LAURA LIBERTY

STRETCH & STRETCH JUNIOR
MICHELE KLINE

LIVING BOUNDARIES

www.ingramcontent.com/pod-product-compliance
Lightning Source LLC
Chambersburg PA
CBHW041429120626

46547CB00002B/143